One Hundred Masterpieces from the Courtauld Collections

Courtauld Institute Galleries

University of London

100 MASTERPIECES
Bernardo Daddi to Ben Nicholson

European Paintings and Drawings
from the 14th to the 20th Century

Illustrated in Colour

Edited by Dennis Farr

Sponsored by Harry Neal Ltd

Published by the Courtauld Institute of Art Fund
London

The (softback) cover shows a detail from
A Bar at the Folies-Bergère by Edouard Manet

© Copyright 1987 The Courtauld Institute of Art Fund

Distributed to the book trade by
Lund Humphries Publishers Ltd
16 Pembridge Road, London W11 3HL

British Library Cataloguing in Publication Data
100 Masterpieces from the Courtauld Collections
1. Painting, European
I. Farr, Dennis
759.94   ND450
ISBN 0–85331–535–3
ISBN 0–85331–534–5 Pbk
Designed by Graham Johnson
Printed by Balding + Mansell UK Limited

The Courtauld Collections

The Courtauld Institute of Art was established in 1931 and became a Senate Institute of the University of London, devoted to the study of the history of art, where the subject could be read to honours level for a first degree. Apart from the Watson Gordon Chair of Fine Art at Edinburgh University, established in 1880, where art history was taken as a joint honours subject, the Courtauld was the first institute in England to offer such a course. There was also provision for postgraduate study for higher degrees, and the first students were welcomed in temporary quarters at 4 Adelphi Terrace, in autumn 1932. Named after our principal benefactor, Samuel Courtauld (1876–1947), chairman of the multinational firm of rayon (synthetic silk) manufacturers, it owed its inspiration in part to the Fogg Art Museum at Harvard University. It is intriguing to reflect that the great art historian and first Director of the National Gallery, Sir Charles Eastlake, twice refused an invitation from the University to become a professor of art history, first in 1833, and again in 1836. This at a time when chairs in the subject were being established at the universities of Berlin (in 1844) and Vienna (1852).

Since 1932, when Courtauld gave us the first group of Impressionist and Post-Impressionist pictures from his collection, the Courtauld's collections have grown and we now have in our care works of art comparable in quality to those at the Ashmolean and Fitzwilliam Museums in Oxford and Cambridge; and our old master drawings collections are probably the finest in the country after those in the British Museum, the Ashmolean and the Royal Collection. Almost all of them have come to us either by gift or bequest, and we have been exceedingly fortunate in our benefactors.

The initiative for founding the Courtauld Institute had originally come from Arthur Lee, 1st Viscount Lee of Fareham (1868–1947), a soldier, diplomat, and politician of great drive and determination, who had served as a military attaché in the United States, and married the daughter of an American banker. He and his wife had given their country home, Chequers, and an art collection to the nation in 1921 for the use of British Prime Ministers. Lee subsequently began a second collection that he bequeathed to the Courtauld in 1947. Although his widow had a life-interest in it, she relinquished ownership upon the opening of the Courtauld Institute Galleries in 1958.

Lord Lee, encouraged by the lawyer, Sir Robert Witt (1872–1952), himself a noted collector of old master drawings, held preliminary negotiations with London University in 1928, and in November of that year a working party was set up under Lee's chairmanship to discuss the academic curriculum and organization of the new institute. Sufficient progress was made so that Lee felt he could approach a likely benefactor to endow the embryo institute. In August 1929 he wrote to Samuel Courtauld outlining his scheme and seeking Courtauld's help. He found Courtauld receptive, for his proposals corresponded to an as yet unformulated idea in Courtauld's own mind. From what we know about Courtauld, from his writings and from those who knew him, he envisaged the study of the history of art as part of a larger humanistic discipline and not simply as arid connoisseurship. When Mrs. Courtauld died in December 1931, Courtauld made over the remaining 50-year lease of his house at 20 Portman Square (Home House) to the university for the use of the Courtauld Institute. Home House is one of Robert Adam's finest town houses, built in 1773–5.

Courtauld's own career as a collector began in 1921, the same year he became chairman of the family firm. His background was, in some respects, that of a conventional, prosperous merchant family who had become landowners in the mid-19th century. He went to Rugby School, but did not proceed to university. Being destined for the family business, he was sent to Lyons and Krefeld to widen his technical knowledge. His family were descended, on his father's side, from Huguenot silversmiths and, latterly, silk-weavers, who had fled France after the Revocation of the Edict of Nantes in 1685. By 1690, Augustin Courtauld and his family had settled in London. On his mother's side, Courtauld could count the poet-banker and collector Samuel Rogers, and the classical scholar Samuel Sharpe, among his forbears. The arts were respected rather than actively cultivated, although Samuel's father, Sydney, played the violin. As a boy Samuel was taken to the National Gallery and the summer exhibitions of the Royal Academy. He later recalled how depressing he found the National Gallery (although in 1936, by a nice irony, he became chairman of the National Gallery Trustees), much preferring the Royal Academy, which he thought more fun, if less serious. Yet the Courtaulds, who had become Unitarians, were set apart by their religious beliefs from their neighbours, and one may speculate that Samuel Courtauld's own interest in the arts was, in part, a reaction against the somewhat puritan mode of family life. He always retained a strong interest in social problems, and in this respect shared the preoccupation of many leading Nonconformist and Quaker families. He also had a strong sense of public duty, and his benefactions were made not for any self-aggrandisement, but for the public good. (He refused a peerage in the Coronation Honours of 1937.)

Courtauld's interest in the Impressionists took a long time to germinate. He and his wife had honeymooned in Italy in 1901, and his understanding of the old masters had deepened as a result of his travels abroad. However, Roger Fry's two epoch-making Post-Impressionist exhibitions, in London, of 1910 and 1912, seem to have left him unmoved. Indeed, his scorn for the Fauves, for example, impeded his appreciation of late-19th-century French painting. It was not until the late Sir Hugh Lane's collection was shown at the Tate Gallery in 1917 that Courtauld received 'his second real "eye-opener",' as he put it, and the final impetus did not come until 1922 when he saw an exhibition of French art at the Burlington Fine Arts Club. Here, 71 works by the greatest artists of the past hundred years were assembled: Corot, Daumier, and Delacroix; Courbet, Manet, and Degas; through to Renoir, Cézanne, Gauguin, and Seurat. Many of the paintings had been lent by Miss Gwendoline Davies, one of the pioneer collectors of Impressionism in Britain.

Courtauld deserves acclaim as a collector, not because he was an innovator, but by his single-minded pursuit of excellence and dynamic acquisition. Within the space of some 10 years he had purchased major works by Degas, Renoir, Manet, Monet, Cézanne, Gauguin, Seurat, Pissarro, and Toulouse-Lautrec. Degas had attracted his approval in about 1910–12, and in this he reflected English taste of the time; but by 1922 he had begun to feel the 'magic' of Cézanne. There can be little doubt that his taste was shaped, to some degree, by the advocacy of Roger Fry. No fewer than 12 Cézannes and 12 Seurats were acquired by Courtauld, either for his own collection, or for the Tate Gallery with the £50,000 he donated in 1923 for the purchase of Impressionist and Post-Impressionist paintings. Outstanding among the early acquisitions from the Tate's Courtauld Fund was Seurat's *Une Baignade, Asnières*, purchased in 1924.

Courtauld and his wife Elizabeth (who was also keenly interested in music) made their first important purchase in 1925, when they bought Renoir's *La Loge*, which had been shown in the first Paris Impressionist exhibition in 1874. Typically, this work combines seductive painterly qualities with significant historical associations, and although Courtauld's response to paintings was strongly emotional rather than coolly intellectual, he nevertheless did not ignore the wider historical context in which they were produced. Thus, in 1926, when Manet's last great masterpiece, *A Bar at the Folies-Bergère* (1881–2), became available, he snapped it up. This splendid picture, full of deliberate spatial and iconic ambiguities, was shown at the Paris Salon of 1882 and is the greatest work in a collection of very fine quality.

Samuel Courtauld's munificence encouraged other benefactions during his own lifetime and subsequent to it. Roger Fry died in 1934, and in accordance with his wishes, his family gave the Courtauld Institute Fry's collection of Bloomsbury Group artists (Duncan Grant, Vanessa Bell, and some Omega Workshops furniture and designs), as well as works by Bonnard, Derain, and Marchand. A few splendid West African carved heads and a wooden bowl in the shape of a bird were also presented.

In 1952 Sir Robert Witt not only bequeathed his extensive photographic archive (on which the Frick Art Reference Library, New York is, in part, based), but also his collection of some 4,000 old master drawings. These he collected less on the principle of 'all the great names' so much as documentary evidence of signed work by little-known artists, or unusual aspects of the work of the great artists. Or even of neglected first-raters, such as Guercino, whose beautiful red chalk *Aurora*, a study for the famous Casino Ludovisi in Rome, was acquired at a time, in the 1930s, when 17th-century art was little sought after. Witt's means were relatively limited, but he still managed to buy many drawings of great beauty.

Other collections were given, including Lord Lee's of 1947, mentioned earlier; and an important bequest came in 1966 from Mark Gambier-Parry of late trecento and quattrocento Italian 'gold-ground' pictures. Formed by his grandfather, Thomas Gambier Parry, in the mid-19th century, the Gambier-Parry collection is an important landmark in the history of taste. The so-called Italian 'primitives' had long been neglected in favour of High Renaissance artists until collectors such as William Roscoe and the Reverend Walter Davenport Bromley began to interest themselves in this period, encouraged by the painter and dealer William Young Ottley.

There were no drawings in this collection, however, and the Courtauld's next major drawings gift and bequest came in 1967 from Mr. and Mrs. W.W. Spooner, who specialized in the English school of watercolourists of the 18th and early 19th centuries. Among the artists represented by fine examples are Alexander and John Robert Cozens, Gainsborough, Richard Wilson, Francis Towne, Girtin, Cotman, and Paul Sandby.

Then, in 1974, Sir Stephen Courtauld's family gave thirteen watercolours by J.M.W. Turner which spanned the artist's career from his early topographical works to the full-blooded romanticism of *Dawn after the Wreck* (c.1841). Both this and a beautifully atmospheric view of *Colchester* (c.1825–6) are reproduced in this book, and we see how Turner transformed the topographical mode into a lyrical vision of acutely observed phenomena, of the effect of early morning sunlight breaking through the winter mist which envelops the town.

But by far the most important bequest since Samuel Courtauld's foundation gifts and bequest to the Courtauld Institute was received in 1978, when Count Antoine Seilern's superb collection of old master paintings and drawings entered our stewardship as the Princes Gate Collection, named after the London house Seilern had lived in for many years after the war. Count Seilern did not want his name overtly associated with the collection, and this condition, stated in his will, was accompanied by others, one of which prevents the Courtauld from lending any of his drawings to locations outside London. Seilern's taste was formed by the Kunsthistorisches Museum, Vienna, and his collection is strong in 15th- and 16th-century Netherlandish artists, masters of the Italian Renaissance, and Rubens. However, it should be added that he had remarkably catholic sympathies, which embraced 18th-century artists such as G.B. Tiepolo and the principal French masters of the 19th century, as well as Picasso and Oskar Kokoschka, from whom he commissioned three large decorative paintings, the *Prometheus Triptych*, in 1950, for the anteroom of his house at 56 Princes Gate.

Of the 300 or so drawings in the Princes Gate Collection, some 20 are reproduced here, including works by Hugo van der Goes, Bellini, Mantegna, Michelangelo, Pieter Bruegel the Elder, Rubens, and Rembrandt. There are also some surprises for those who think of Courtauld as primarily a collector of late 19th-century French art, for the Tiepolo *Holy Family* which is discussed here, belonged to him. Nor have the Courtauld Collections stopped short at the art of the 1920s. Recently, Dr. Alastair Hunter bequeathed a choice group of paintings from which a Ben Nicholson and an Ivon Hitchens are included in this volume, as well as works by Graham Sutherland, Keith Vaughan, John Hoyland, Prunella Clough, Patrick Heron, Hans Hartung, and Paul Nash, and a small sculpture by César. Lillian Browse, the former London art dealer, has generously given and promised us the greater part of her collection of late 19th- and early 20th-century French and British art, together with some paintings by living British artists. Thus the collections continue to grow and to reflect the art of our own day.

This book is both a celebration and an invitation: we honour our benefactors by discussing the work of some of the great artists represented in the collections they have given, and we hope that by focusing on 100 outstanding masterpieces, the reader's enjoyment and understanding will be deepened when looking at the works themselves.

Dennis Farr   *June 1987*
Director, Courtauld Institute Galleries

Acknowledgments

This publication owes its existence to the generous sponsorship of Harry Neal Ltd, through the keen support of Mr. H. Morton Neal, who is also Chairman of the Executive Appeal Committee for the Courtauld Institute of Art Fund. We are most grateful to him and his firm, as we are also to the Business Sponsorship Incentive Scheme, operating under the aegis of A.B.S.A., who made a matching grant of £25,000 towards this publication.

As editor, I am much indebted to those of my colleagues at the Courtauld who gave up precious time to contribute essays on the 100 paintings and drawings featured in this book. A list of contributors appears below, each of whom can be identified by their initials at the end of each essay.

I gratefully acknowledge Mr. Paul Cummings, who as Editor of *Drawing* (The International Review published by The Drawing Society, New York), allowed me to use an edited version of my article on the Courtauld Collections which first appeared in vol. VIII, No.5 (January–February 1987) of that publication. I am grateful to Mr. John Nicoll of Yale University Press for allowing us to publish edited versions of notes on our Impressionist paintings, which featured in the exhibition catalogue *Impressionist & Post-Impressionist Masterpieces: The Courtauld Collection* (1987).

For valuable assistance on aspects of drawing techniques I thank Mr. William Bradford and Mr. William Clarke. The book has been designed by Mr. Graham Johnson, and the colour photography was carried out by A.C. Cooper Ltd.   D.F.

Proceeds from the sale of this book will go to the Courtauld Institute of Art Fund, and help to finance the move of both the Institute and the Galleries to the North Block of Somerset House.

100 Masterpieces from the Courtauld Collections

Drawings

Editorial Note

The book has been divided into two main sections: paintings, followed by drawings and watercolours (including pastels). The sequence is broadly chronological, beginning with the Bernardo Daddi triptych of 1338, the earliest dated work in the collection. Where several works by the same artist are reproduced, the sequence is again chronological; thus of the five paintings by Rubens included here, the *Descent from the Cross* c.1611 comes first, followed by the portrait of Jan Breughel and his family, and ending with the magnificent late *Landscape by Moonlight* of 1635–40.

All dimensions are given in centimetres, height before width.

A work is unsigned and/or undated, unless otherwise specified.

There is an index of artists, with page references, at the end of the book.

List of Contributors

A.B.	Anita Brookner	J.H.	John House
H.B.	Helen Braham	M.H.	Michael Hirst
W.B.	William Bradford	R.H.	Rupert Hodge
J.C.	Joanna Cannon	T.J.	Tania Jones
L.C.	Lorne Campbell	J.A.N.	John Newman
P.D.	Paul Davies	D.H.S.	David H. Solkin
D.E.	David Ekserdjian	J.S.	John Sunderland
D.F.	Dennis Farr	N.T.	Nonie Tasker
J.F.	Jennifer Fletcher	A.W-L.	Aidan Weston-Lewis
C.G.	Catherine Gordon	J.W.	Joanna Woodall
C.H.	Colum Hourihane	S.W.	Sarah Wilson

Bernardo Daddi (recorded from 1327, died 1348)

Triptych: The Virgin and Child Enthroned with Saints and Angels;
above, *The Redeemer* (centre);
The Nativity, The Crucifixion, The Four Evangelists, The Annunciation
(inside of wings);
The Adoration of the Magi, Two Bishop Saints (outside of wings)   1338

Tempera on panel. Max. height: 87.5;
width at base: 42; wings: 62 (max.) × 17.
Dated 1338 on base: '·ANNO·DNI[M]·CCC·XXXVIII'.
Princes Gate Collection

The
triptych
closed

This triptych is an exquisite example of the portable tabernacle produced for private patrons in 14th-century Italy. Because its physical structure and paint surface are remarkably well preserved, it is possible to gauge the work's original effect and use. Standing in the home or taken on a journey, the triptych would be opened for prayer and meditation, and then, when closed again, admired for the scene which, in this sole surviving example, is painted on the outside of the shutters. Long, detailed, and repeated contemplation of each image was possible. The density and richness of the tabernacle's surface decoration, and of its religious content, rewarded this close attention.

The surface shimmers with gold. Burnished and stamped leaf fills the backgrounds, while filaments of leaf, applied to the bright egg-tempera paint surface, embellish the undulating hem of the Virgin's mantle, lend the appearance of rich brocade to the material on the throne back, or describe the highlights on the individual feathers of Gabriel's wings. The panel's closely packed images constitute a compendium of major Christian truths presented in the form of detailed narratives. Meditation on the Nativity, for instance, would be enlivened by observing the tender communication between Mother and Child shown here. Reciprocal glances and gestures recur as a motif throughout the triptych. Gabriel's salutation to the Virgin and her hesitant response link the two separate parts of the Annunciation scene which crown the inner faces of the shutters on either side of the central panel. On the reverse of these shutters are two images which, when the tabernacle is closed, unite to form the scene of the Adoration of the Magi. On the left wing two of the Magi gaze and gesture towards the star beyond the central framing moulding. Turning this interruption to advantage, the artist continues the rocky landscape beyond the frame, creating the illusion of a single scene, witnessed through a pair of arched windows.

The triptych is attributed to the Florentine artist Bernardo Daddi, and the date 1338 is inscribed on its plinth. This falls neatly in the middle of Daddi's known oeuvre since his earliest surviving work is the Ognissanti triptych of 1328 while his last signed and dated work is the S. Giorgio a Ruballa polyptych of 1348, also in the Courtauld's collections, painted in the year of his death. Daddi, who felt the influence of both Giotto and of his Sienese contemporaries, appears to have run a well-organised and prolific workshop, specialising in panel paintings, many of them devotional tabernacles. The Princes Gate triptych ranks among the finest of these works, both for the refinement of its execution and for the quality of its narrative invention. J.C.

Lorenzo Monaco (c.1370–c.1425)

The Coronation of the Virgin c.1394–95

Tempera on panel in original frame, 208 × 179
Gambier-Parry Collection

This is the most important remaining element of a substantial triptych that originally adorned the high altar of the Church of S. Gaggio (Caius) in Florence. It and various other parts of the complex were first given to Lorenzo Monaco as recently as 1950 (in a brilliant article by H.D. Gronau), and the subsequent identification of yet more fragments of the altarpiece has only tended to confirm the attribution. The work probably dates from about 1394–5, that is to say before Lorenzo became a Camaldolensian monk, and is one of his earliest surviving productions. Although Lorenzo originally came from Siena, the style is entirely Florentine, and owes a great deal to the example of Agnolo Gaddi, the leading Florentine painter of the period. This is apparent not only in the facial types of the figures, both the delicate blond angels and the decidedly more vigorous Christ, but also in the colour-scheme. Thus, while the bold reds and blues of Christ and God the Father – shown blessing and holding an open book inscribed with the Greek letters Alpha and Omega in the trefoil above the main scene – are conventional enough, the subtler tones of the Virgin's draperies and the pale yellows, pinks, and greens of the angels underline the influence of Agnolo. These colours are repeated across the picture surface, and complement the conscious symmetry of the composition. The Coronation of the Virgin often served as the focus for a great company of Saints in Florentine art, but here in the pinnacle the approach is more intimate, in spite of the grandeur of the two-seater Gothic throne, its form cleverly adapted to the shape of the panel, and the richness of the Oriental cloth of honour with its lapis lazuli and orange pattern of birds and flowers. Similarly, both opulence and attention to detail are perfectly balanced in the gilded and patterned haloes, each one of which is unique. Finally, it is worth noting the empirical as opposed to scientific attempt at perspective in the recession of the floor tiles, as well as the way the foremost angels lead us into the picture.   D.E.

Fra Angelico (c.1395/1400–1455)

Predella: A Dominican Saint, S. Dorothy (left panel);
S. Mary Magdalen, The Dead Christ, S. John the Evangelist (centre panel);
S. Catherine of Alexandria, S. Agnes (right panel)

Tempera on panel, respectively: 20.3 × 49.4; 20.3 × 54.5; 20.3 × 50.7
Gambier-Parry Collection

These three panels originally formed a single horizontal band. This is the characteristic shape of a predella, the base section of a multi-panelled altarpiece. It served to support the principal parts of the painting, both literally and metaphorically. The predella formed a stable foundation which raised the panel, making it more visible to the onlooker, and it was decorated with small-scale scenes or, as in this case, figures, which provided an additional commentary on the main images above.

Recent opinion has been unanimous in associating the paintings with the name of Fra Angelico, either attributing the works to his shop, or to the master himself. This lack of certainty is not surprising: the execution of a large altarpiece was generally divided between a number of artists, and the predella, while providing the opportunity for virtuoso painting on a small scale, was not the most important section. The inclusion at the left end of the predella of a Dominican Saint is perhaps not suprising, given Angelico's membership of that order. The fact that this is a nun is less expected and, taken together with the inclusion of four other female Saints on the predella, suggests that our panels once belonged to an altarpiece made for a house of Dominican nuns. Since the style of the panels is now usually placed early in Angelico's maturity a convincing case has been made for connecting them with the *Virgin and Child with Dominican Saints*, now in the Museo di S. Marco, Florence, painted for the Dominican nuns of S. Pietro Martire, Florence, before March 1429.

The image of Christ as the Man of Sorrows, flanked by the lance and sponge, originally appeared directly below the Virgin and Child of the main panel, reminding the onlooker of the sufferings to come. The reactions of Mary Magdalen and S. John guided the spectator's response, and the emotional pitch was heightened by the contrast between the green tones of Christ's flesh, the vibrant orange-red of the Magdalen's garment, and the pink with a blue cast used for the Evangelist's mantle. The counterpoint of bright hues found throughout the garments in the predella provided a lively note below the sombre habits of the Dominican Saints in the main panel. The care with which these small panels were executed is evident in many details: the delicacy of S. Agnes' right hand as she holds both lamb and palm; the heightened flush of S. John's cheek and temple; the individual curling strands of the Magdalen's hair. J.C.

Master of Flémalle (? Robert Campin, c.1375–1444)

Triptych: The Entombment (centre panel); Two Thieves with the Empty Cross and a Donor; The Resurrection (wings) c.1420

Panel, centre 60 × 48.9, each wing 60 × 22.5
Princes Gate Collection

In the left wing, though Christ's body has been removed from the central Cross, the thieves remain in torment on their crosses. The donor kneels in the foreground; a book hangs in a cloth cover between his hands; no trace of an inscription can be found on the scroll next to his head. In the centre panel, the body of Christ is lowered into the tomb by Joseph of Arimathea and Nicodemus. The Virgin, supported by S. John, leans over to kiss Christ; the other women are the Three Maries. Four angels, two hovering and two standing, carry the Instruments of the Passion: the spear, Crown of Thorns, nails and sponge. In the right wing, the resurrected Christ, watched by an angel, steps from the tomb, which is guarded by three soldiers. Two are asleep, while the third is astonished into consciousness. The boldly patterned draperies suggest an eastern setting and the gilded backgrounds, bearing differing, raised patterns of vine tendrils, leaves and grapes, relate the subject-matter to the mysteries of the Eucharist. The frames are original.

The donor cannot be identified and nothing is known about the early history of the triptych. Apparently too small to have been used as an altar-piece, it may have been displayed in the donor's house. On stylistic grounds, the triptych is attributed to the Master of Flémalle, who painted the panels of the *Virgin and Child* and *S. Veronica* allegedly from Flémalle near Liège and now at Frankfurt. He was very possibly Robert Campin, a leading Tournai painter, and the triptych seems to be his earliest surviving work. The donor's costume may indicate that it was painted in about 1420. The artist has evidently used an oil-based medium, though one less tractable than that of Campin's contemporary Jan van Eyck. It has allowed him to render a wide range of tones and his boldness in juxtaposing strongly contrasting tones and his accuracy in depicting all the subtle tonal transitions in the flesh and draperies allow his figures to appear startlingly convincing. He is able to reproduce well-defined facial expressions and dramatically eloquent gestures. The colours, carefully balanced, and the striking linear patterns contribute to the powerful decorative and expressive effect of the triptych, one of the first and greatest masterpieces of Early Netherlandish painting. L.C.

Attributed to Rogier van der Weyden (c.1399–1464)

Portrait of a Man (? Guillaume Fillastre);
verso: *Branch of Holly*

Panel, 33.7 × 23.5
Inscribed on the frame: 'IE HE CE QVE MORD';
on the reverse of the frame: 'Ie he ce que mord'

Accepted by H.M. Treasury in lieu of capital taxation, and allocated to the Home House Society on behalf of the Courtauld Institute Galleries, 1987.

verso

Though sadly damaged, the portrait is interesting because of its highly original composition, its decorated reverse, which is in better condition, and its frame. Moreover the sitter has been plausibly identified as Guillaume Fillastre, who died in 1473. The illegitimate son of a Cardinal, he was Bishop successively of Verdun, Toul and Tournai, Abbot of Saint-Bertin at St Omer and Chancellor of the Order of the Golden Fleece. A powerful figure at the court of the Dukes of Burgundy, he was an important author and patron of the arts. The motto painted on the frame, interpreted as meaning 'I hate that which I sting', may be connected with the holly on the reverse, but no other instance has been discovered of Fillastre's use of this device and this motto. Fixed into the top of the frame is an iron attachment which is possibly original and which could have been used for hanging the picture – perhaps from a long chain so that it could have been turned to show the reverse – or for sliding it into and out of a protective case.

Fillastre became Bishop of Verdun in 1437 and it has been proposed that the portrait, where he appears in academic(?) dress, was painted before that date. Bishops, however, were not invariably represented wearing copes and the portrait may be later. Its damaged condition makes it impossible to judge the sitter's age. It is usually attributed to Rogier van der Weyden. The sitter is depicted looking up almost casually from his book. The implied spontaneous movement of the scholar interrupted while reading is quite unlike the very formal and static poses of Rogier's sitters. Rogier was a superb draughtsman who gave much thought to elegance of linear design, whereas the painter of this portrait was neither an outstanding draughtsman nor much concerned with linear harmonies. He was perhaps an associate of Rogier and developed in a rather different way upon the example set by the Master of Flémalle in his portraits. Such experiments in the informal presentation of the sitter were not to be seen again in the Netherlands until Quinten Massys' portraits of the early years of the 16th century.

This painting was formerly in the collection of Sir Thomas Merton.   L.C.

Alessandro Filipepi, called Il Botticelli (c.1444–1510)

The Trinity with S. Mary Magdalen and S. John the Baptist, the Archangel Raphael and Tobias c.1491–94

Tempera on panel, 214.9 × 191.2
Lee Collection

This picture is almost certainly the main panel of the high altarpiece of the Augustinian convent of Sant'Elisabetta delle Convertite in Florence, which was founded in 1329 to house penitent prostitutes. The work's destination explains the prominence of Mary Magdalen on the right hand of the Trinity, and it is her legend that forms the subject of the predella, now in the John G. Johnson Collection at the Philadelphia Museum of Art. As part of the construction of a new church, building work on the chapel that contained the high altarpiece was begun in 1491, and the church and its altars were completed by Christmas 1494. Botticelli probably painted his picture around this time, as its style would also suggest, and may well have been paid with money provided by a lay patron. The condition of the work makes it hard to determine its autograph status, and while it is universally accepted that the design is the invention of the master, opinions differ as to the extent of workshop participation in the execution.

This type of representation of the Trinity, with Christ Crucified at its centre, known as the Throne of Mercy, was not unusual in Florentine art of the period, and was often accompanied as here by attendant Saints and cherubim. Botticelli concentrates on the physical sufferings of Christ, and on the intense emotion felt by God the Father, no longer a remote patriarch but rather a lamenting human presence full of pathos, and by Mary Magdalen. Her worn features and long, shaggy hair mark her as a sinner who has repented, rapt in adoration of the mystery of the Trinity, while John the Baptist, the patron Saint of Florence, looks out of the picture to engage our attention, and to encourage us to contemplate the central vision, as recommended by Leon'Battista Alberti in his theoretical treatise, *On Painting*. The barren and rocky landscape is an entirely appropriate setting for both Saints, as also for the journey of Raphael and Tobias, who are shown in front of the other figures and on a much smaller scale, and may have been included at the behest of the altarpiece's principal patron. The picture's dull colour is somewhat deceptive, because brighter reds and blues would be revealed by cleaning, but it must always have been a passionate and tragic work, and the expressive energy of Botticelli's line is never in doubt. D.E.

Quinten Massys (1466–1530)

The Madonna Standing with the Child and Angels

Oil on panel, 47.5 × 33
Princes Gate Collection

Few contemporary references exist to Quinten Massys' early career as an artist apart from the fact that he entered the St Luke Guild of Painters in Antwerp in 1491. This city was to remain his home, with the exception of a possible visit or visits to Italy, until his death at the age of 64. To compensate for this shortage of early biographical details there is a wealth of later anecdotal information and legends surrounding this artist. Facts such as his early career as a smith, his friends and associates and the decoration of his house have been embellished with the passage of time.

His earliest works, dated to c.1491–1507, are small iconic images of various Saints and representations of the Madonna and Child, such as the example in the National Gallery, London. The two commissions for the S. Anne Altarpiece (1507–9; Brussels, Musées Royaux) and the S. John Altarpiece (1508–11; Antwerp, Koninklijk Museum) not only constitute a turning point in his career but also reflect a change in iconography.

With the possible exception of this Madonna and Child, Massys was to forsake the earlier and standard iconic image until the last decade of his career. Nothing is known of the original ownership of this work or of the copy now in Lyons Museum, but it is generally agreed that the present example is the earliest and was probably painted between 1500 and 1509 for a wealthy donor for private worship. Cult images of the Madonna were popular in 15th- and 16th-century Netherlands and from such precedents Massys borrows significantly. Whereas Massys' central positioning of the Madonna and Child beneath the vestibule arch is given an Italianate element by the presence of putti with garlands and swags, features which echo the work of Hans Memlinc, his architectural context is paralleled in a simplified format in the early 15th-century work of Jan van Eyck and Robert Campin. Massys' distorted use of perspective is matched by his equally unusual positioning of portal figures representing Old Testament Prophet figures, in a context in which they would never be found in reality. Similarly, the wooded landscape, immediately behind the Madonna's head, on the right hand side is an unlikely element, the basis for which lies in Massys' innovative style. Another element borrowed from van Eyck and Campin is the angelic support to the Madonna. Here they are shown playing a lute, another with a possibly bowed instrument, a third offering a flower and yet another in the background preparing a throne, the canopy of which carries an inscription '. . . us' and 'Maria'. The emphasis throughout the picture, from the finely painted halo to the lofty architectural setting, the attendant angels and the preparation of the throne, is on the majesty of the Madonna. Another example of this artist's work, *Christ on the Cross, between the Virgin, S. John and Two Donors* and dating to the early 1490s is in the Princes Gate Collection.

C.H.

Ascribed to Giovanni Bellini (c.1430–1516)

The Assassination of S. Peter Martyr ?1509

Oil on panel, 67.3 × 100.4
Lee Collection

This work is attributed to Giovanni Bellini because it closely resembles a painting of the same subject ascribed to him in the National Gallery, London. It is impossible to check the date 1509 that is reported to have once been visible on the back of the panel as this is now covered with a recent blind cradle. The original function and location are unknown since the picture is first recorded with a Viennese dealer in 1910 but its size and exquisite detail indicate a close-up view in a connoisseur's collection or some Dominican Prior's cell. A clue to the patron's identity may be provided by the arms (a suitably cruel bird of prey) on the soldier's shield. This soldier is significantly absent from the National Gallery picture and as he is superfluous to the story and the action, his rôle and striped stockings are probably heraldic. Devotion to Peter Martyr was strong in the Veneto for he was born at Verona. In Venice a lay confraternity propagated his cult by commissioning pictures of his martyrdom. By the early 16th century the city owned several bits of his body and the bleeding trees could relate to a relic of his blood.

The story is told in the *Golden Legend*. In 1252 the Dominican Saint was ambushed between Como and Milan by assassins hired by local heretics. Peter's companion Brother Dominic though mortally wounded escaped. Peter brought to his knees by an axe blow to the head was despatched by a dagger to the body. Dying he reaffirmed his Christian belief by writing 'credo' with his blood in the dust. The painter had added telling details. The Saint's cutting down is paralleled with the action of the woodmen felling trees which bleed in sympathy. The buttercup (?) blooming prominently in the foreground may be inspired by those flowers in Ovid's *Metamorphoses* which spring from the blood of dying youths loved by the gods and so guarantees their immortality.

The picture is composed of two wooden panels which have split where they join causing some damage horizontally across the centre. The brown border is a later addition. The paint is applied thinly with small strokes from fine brushes and extensive finger printing suggests some working by hand towards a softer focus. The foliage and the grass were once greener. Infra-red examination has revealed many *pentimenti*, the most interesting being the widening of the central gap in the trees and the suppression of a small man standing there beside a horse. The tree trunks were painted in first and show through all the foreground figures except for the left-hand soldier. There are no substantial alterations to those four figures which so closely resemble the principal characters in the National Gallery picture, and this taken with the possibility that the wood in our painting may have also once been continuous, makes it highly likely that our painter working under Bellini's supervision from his master's picture has rearranged its main elements, enlarged the figure scale, invented a soldier and added details like the books, spurs, hound and fallen shield. The result is a painting of very high quality in which the relationship between figure and landscape is less subtle than in a Bellini but more sensational.

J.F.

Mariotto Albertinelli (1474–1515)

The Creation c.1513–15

Oil on panel, 56.5 × 165.5
Gambier-Parry Collection

The Creation, one of a series of three panels of uniform height by Albertinelli depicting scenes from the book of Genesis (the others show the *Expulsion from Paradise* and *Cain and Abel*), may be one of the three *storiette* (little narratives) said by Vasari to have been painted for Giovanni Maria Benintendi after the election of Leo X as Pope, which took place in 1513. The long low format is reminiscent of the type of chest used for wedding linen called a *cassone*, and it seems likely that the picture originally formed part of a piece of furniture. As often happened with *cassone* paintings, it observes the by this date distinctly old-fashioned convention of representing a number of different scenes from the one story within the same picture field and in a continuous landscape. Reading from left to right, the episodes proceed chronologically, beginning with the Creation of the Animals, the Creation of Adam, the Creation of Eve, and ending with the Temptation and Fall.

The Creation of the Animals allows the artist to indulge in a parade of exotic creatures, including a camel and an elephant, as well as a rearing horse inspired by the antique, but all this exuberant detail is kept well in the background. Man is the true subject of the painting, and dominates it. His

creation is eminently physical, as God the Father – long-bearded but not old – pulls him into existence, while two angels fly overhead, one pointing out the scene and the other joining his hands in prayer. Here, as in the Temptation, Adam's pose is derived from a classical model, and indeed the painting is full of references to ancient statues and reliefs. Next comes the Creation of Eve out of Adam's side as he slumbers: in this episode a mere gesture of benediction suffices, and Eve emerges, hands joined in prayer, supported by the same two angels. In the final scene, the Tree of the Knowledge of Good and Evil closes the composition, as Eve hands Adam a split fig from its laden branches, while the insidious human-faced serpent whispers encouragement in her ear. All the way across the picture profiles predominate, occasionally interspersed with more frontal views, and in spite of the potentially dramatic events enacted, the mood remains tranquil throughout. Mariotto Albertinelli, who was a close collaborator of Fra Bartolommeo, is reported by Vasari to have given up painting in favour of inn-keeping; be that as it may, his great gifts as an artist are amply demonstrated by this particular work. The landscape, bisected by the serene river flowing out into the distance, is exceptionally fine. D.E.

Girolamo Francesco Maria Mazzola, called Parmigianino (1503–1540)

The Holy Family c.1523

Oil on panel, 43.1 × 47.3; pictorial area: 37.5 × 42.2
Princes Gate Collection

Francesco Mazzola is generally known by his nickname, Parmigianino, after his native city, Parma. A precocious artist, he soon came under the influence of Correggio, the major painter then working in the city. By the time he left for Rome in 1524, at the age of 21, he had already produced a body of paintings in oil and in fresco of impressive quality.

This intimate little nativity scene is depicted with the serenity and charm which is particularly associated with Correggio's art. It was probably painted about 1523, and shows a likeness to Parmigianino's frescoes of Diana and Actaeon at Fontanellato, near Parma. A foretaste of interests he would find in Rome, however, is provided by the evident use for the Christ Child's pose of an engraving after Raphael's fresco of *Galatea* in the Farnesina in Rome.

The small scale is unusual for Parmigianino. Beneath the frame is a border of about 2.7cm. of completely unpainted wood, the purpose of which is far from apparent. Until recent times a heavily tinted yellow varnish had coated the painting and was probably the cause of the divergence of opinion about its authorship. In the blue mantle around the Virgin the artist's pigment, probably lapis lazuli, has deteriorated, and strengthening has been added later to the folds, as well as an overall glaze. Similarly misleading is the discoloration of copper resinate used for the feathery foliage on the left and as a glaze for the vine-cladding of the portico, over malachite, of which pigment the original green colour now shows through the wing of the caressing angel.

Underdrawing – perhaps in chalk – is visible to the naked eye, and more clearly with infra-red rays; this drawing is not consistently followed, the artist changing images when painting them in. Between the Virgin's face and the angel's wing appears the drawing of another angel's face, and X-rays indicate that paint was wiped away here. The Child's slightly differing position of head and limbs, the raised arm of S. Joseph, the ox's lower position, can all be seen in underdrawing. The Virgin's profile is altered and her pose probably turned more fully away from us – indeed a much more radical alteration may have taken place here. A number of surviving drawings may belong to an earlier stage in the evolution of the design; Parmigianino was a prolific draughtsman and, later increasingly so, extraordinarily painstaking in his designs.

The disparity between a certain sentimentality in the animals and the angel and the monumental gravity of the architectural setting and of the S. Joseph which hint of things to come, is a reminder that this is the work of a youth barely 20 years old.   H.B.

34

Girolamo Francesco Maria Mazzola, called Parmigianino (1503–1540)

The Virgin and Child c.1524–27

Oil on panel, 63.5 × 50.7
Princes Gate Collection

The Virgin and Child has generally been dated to Parmigianino's stay in Rome from 1524 to 1527. Indeed, the classical building in the background appears to be an evocation of one of the sights of ancient Rome, the Septizonium, an impressive ruin soon to be demolished in 1588 (the same background appears later in a drawing of the *Visitation*). The pose of the Virgin may well have been inspired by the figure of the Erythraean Sibyl in one of the great modern sights of Rome, Michelangelo's ceiling in the Sistine Chapel. Above all, we see here, succeeding to the charm of Correggio, the gravity of the art of Raphael, who had died in Rome four years before Parmigianino's arrival. It was in particular with Raphael's pupils and artistic circle that the young artist was associated in these years; the impact on his art was profound. His biographer, Vasari, was to write: 'the spirit of Raphael was said afterwards to have passed into the body of Francesco'.

This painting is unfinished and therefore gives an intimate view of Parmigianino at work. The artist has completed the background architecture and brilliant blue sky with a freedom of handling, beautifully clear because of its good condition, which distinguishes it from the little *Holy Family*. Comparison of the X-rays of the two paintings shows, however, that the underlying blocking-in of the composition is as broadly handled there as it is here. The curtain must be almost finished; to the Virgin and her Child the finishing touches were still to come, while the intended blue of the Virgin's mantle can only be guessed at; the still-exposed dark brown ground fills the right corner. Most interestingly, Parmigianino has left unsolved the arrangement of the Virgin's legs; they were both evidently first planned outstretched, as in a preparatory drawing in the Albertina, Vienna, which the painting follows closely, except for the presence there of an angel. Two visible attempts to position the right leg more supportively in an upright position evidently did not satisfy the artist either.

The unfinished state of the present painting may be due to the artist's flight after the Sack of Rome to Bologna. It was in Bologna that Vasari bought an unfinished painting of a Madonna by Parmigianino that may be our painting. The artist spent the last 10 years of his life mainly in Parma, where he apparently became increasingly eccentric and absorbed in hermeticism and alchemy. The contrived elegance evident in the *Virgin and Child* was to be pursued almost to bizarre abstraction in the artist's quest of a personal ideal beauty. His perfectionism led him to procrastinate to such a degree that he was imprisoned for breach of contract. He escaped and died in exile at the same early age as Raphael. H.B.

Lucas Cranach the Elder (1472–1553)

Adam and Eve 1526

Oil on panel, 117.1 × 80.5
Signed with the winged serpent and dated 1526 on the tree in the centre
Lee Collection

The animals in the Garden of Eden are a stag, a hind, a sheep, a roe-buck, its head reflected in the pool, with its mate, a lion, a wild boar and a horse; the birds are partridges, a stork and a heron. Silhouetted against another tree is the Tree of Knowledge. Around its trunk a grape-vine grows and from its branches the Serpent emerges to tempt Eve, who offers the apple to the perplexed Adam. On the tree trunk are the date 1526 and the bat-winged serpent which formed part of Cranach's coat of arms.

Cranach, who was a close friend of Martin Luther, worked at the court of Saxony. Famous for his landscapes, his representations of animals and his nudes, he found in *Adam and Eve* a subject which was ideally suited to his gifts and to which the Lutherans did not object. He and his workshop treated it many times in paintings and prints.

This painting is influenced by Dürer's celebrated engraving of the same subject, dated 1504. Dürer had also included many animals but, while Dürer's animals may be interpreted as allusions to the Four Humours, Cranach's animals are less solemn and portentous. A related drawing once at Dresden, though closer to Dürer's print, is still less solemn than the painting; there Eve puts the apple into Adam's mouth and Adam holds a phallic apple-branch which both conceals and connects his and Eve's genital organs. The vine, not present in the drawing, refers to the Redemption, so that the picture has some didactic function. While the pairing of the sheep with the lion may have a moral meaning, the association of Adam with the sheep is perhaps intended as a wry comment on Adam's behaviour. The principal purpose of the painting, presumably made for a wealthy collector, is evidently to give pleasure rather than instruction. Cranach holds a balance between highly decorative, stylised forms and an immediacy and liveliness of presentation. The unexpectedly free technique of the foliage and grass is a reminder that Cranach was renowned for his speed of working.   L.C.

Lorenzo Lotto (c.1480–1556)

The Holy Family with Saints Anne and Joachim 1535?

Oil on canvas, 58.5 × 78.9
Signed and dated on the cushion, lower right, 'L. Loto [sic] 153 [5?]'
Princes Gate Collection

Lorenzo di Tommaso Lotto was born in Venice, a near-contemporary of Titian and Giorgione, whose fame somewhat overshadowed his own peripatetic career. Lotto is first documented as working in Treviso in 1503, and by 1506 had moved to the Marche where, already a painter of repute, he was commissioned to paint a polyptych for the church of S. Domenico, Recanati, which he completed in 1508. At the end of 1508 he was in Rome, painting in the Vatican alongside Raphael (although no documented work seems to have survived), before moving back to the Marche in 1512, and establishing himself at Bergamo from 1513–25; he was in Venice by 1526, but spent long periods in the Marche (1534–9) and Treviso (1542–5), and in 1550 tried to auction some of his pictures in Ancona to provide for his old age. He retired in 1552 to the Santa Casa at Loreto, where he died.

This brief account of Lotto's career explains in part why he was regarded as outside the Venetian artistic mainstream, and his achievements underrated. Yet his work has great quality and marked individuality of style. *The Holy Family with Saints Anne and Joachim* is related to the *Virgin and Child with Saints Anne, Joachim and Jerome* (Florence, Uffizi), which is signed and dated 1534. The group of the Virgin and Child and Saint Anne as portrayed in the Uffizi picture, is repeated with a few minor variations in the Princes Gate composition, but in place of Saint Jerome, the artist has substituted a window which looks out on to a delightful hilly landscape. Although this painting is also signed and dated, the last digit is almost illegible, but it has been read as '1535', which would make it the later of the two versions.

It is perhaps significant that Lotto painted this picture soon after a long stay in Venice, and in both colour and composition it is among the most Venetian, and specifically Titianesque, of his works. There is, however, a strong psychological tension present in the almost startled manner in which the Virgin Mary draws back from the fervent adoration displayed by her father, S. Joachim, and his attitude contrasts with calm resignation shown by the Virgin's mother, S. Anne who, hands crossed over her breast, looks down protectively on the group.   D.F.

Master 'A.W.'

Portrait of a Lady 1536

Oil on panel, 76.5 × 60.5
Signed in monogram and dated, upper left: 'AW (?)/ PINGEBAT/ 1536'
Lee Collection

A richly and fashionably dressed lady holds a white rose in her right hand and stands behind a table on which rests a gilded covered cup decorated with figures of classical warriors. The ink-pot, paper, pen and pen-case are not original but are early additions. The sitter wears narrow gold rings on both hands and one ring is inscribed 'IHS' (Jhesus). Her dress, which is dark grey over a red under-painting enhancing its richness of colour, bears a bold black pattern which is now scarcely visible. The frame and the sitter appear to cast shadows across the background. The artist drew the sitter's right hand in a different position, to our left of the painted hand; several objects are not under-drawn and considerable alterations have been made during the course of execution.

Perhaps because the portrait comes from the collection of the Earls of Darnley, and perhaps because the sitter holds a rose reminiscent of the 'White Rose of York', the lady has been identified as a member of the English royal family: either as Queen Mary I or as her cousin Margaret Douglas, Countess of Lennox. The painter's monogram has been read as AW and it has been suggested that he was Andrew Wright, Serjeant Painter to Henry VIII. It is, however, clear that the artist was trained in the Low Countries and that his style and technique are similar to those of such Antwerp portrait-painters as Joos van Cleve. The sitter, evidently a lady of high rank, is not necessarily an Englishwoman; the costume is not specifically English and the lady may be a Netherlander. The covered pot is the usual attribute of S. Mary Magdalen and it is possible that the sitter is masquerading as the Saint. The monogram need not necessarily be read as AW or WA, nor is it necessarily made up of the artist's initials. A similar monogram, inverted, was used by the Netherlandish artists Jacob Cornelisz. and Cornelis Buys II.

L.C.

Pieter Bruegel the Elder (c.1525–69)

Landscape with the Flight into Egypt 1563

Oil on panel, 37.2 × 55.5
Signed and dated, lower right: 'BRUEGEL MDLXIII'
Princes Gate Collection

Bruegel, best known for his representations of outdoor peasant scenes, painted this lyrical landscape with a religious theme in 1563. He painted it soon after his arrival and recent marriage, in Brussels, probably for Cardinal Antoine Perrenot de Granvella, who was then Archbishop of Malines and the following year the President of the Netherlands Council of State, acting as spokesman for Philip II. (The painting is, however, only first recorded in Granvella's collection in the inventory of his home in Besançon in 1607 although it is known he patronised Bruegel throughout his life.)

For Bruegel, this painting was the culmination of his alpine studies, some of which were intended for a series of engravings that he had executed in the preceding decade after his travels to Italy. The subject lends itself to the landscape and was therefore frequently depicted in early Netherlandish painting. Although more sophisticated, it is still evocative of the tradition of Netherlandish and, indeed, German landscape artists of the late 15th and early 16th centuries. It is a panoramic landscape seen from a high viewpoint, embracing a vista of the world which was called 'Weltlandschaft'. The motifs of high mountains, craggy cliffs overlooking dense forests and a low-lying river valley with jutting out hamlets, churches and castles were particularly common features. Bruegel continues the conventional colour scheme to achieve the sense of receding space and spatial unity used by the Antwerp artists, Joachim Patinir, Herri met de Bles and Cornelis Massys, for example. This consisted of shades of brown for the foreground, green for the middle distance, and blue for the background. The colours blend more subtly in this painting and he was to abandon the formula completely in 1565 when he created the famous series of *The Months*. The detail, particularly the foliage and flowers in the right hand corner, is also finer.

In this picture, unlike the more famous of his works, the figures are dominated by the landscape and yet they are significant. Mary is recognised riding on the donkey in her usual deep red cloak. Bruegel has also used traditional symbols for this subject; the idol falling from the willow-trunk on the right signifies the defeat of paganism by the coming of Christ, the two minute salamanders below the Family represent evil. Although in the whole scene a sense of calm prevails, the urgency of the Flight is conveyed by the action of Joseph who, in the exact centre of the picture with his back to us, slightly bent, tugs the animal's halter.

This painting was particularly admired and popular. It was owned first by the painter Sir Peter Paul Rubens and passed to the well-known 17th-century collector Pieter Stevens. T.J.

44

Sir Peter Paul Rubens (1577–1640)

The Descent from the Cross c.1611

Oil on panel, 115 × 76
Lee Collection

It is generally accepted this is the oil sketch for *The Descent from the Cross* that Rubens used to impress the Guild of Harquebusiers and secure the contract to paint their great altarpiece for Antwerp Cathedral. Rubens was formally charged with the commission in September 1611, and the massive central panel, which differs in composition from the preparatory oil sketch in only minor details, was delivered to the Cathedral a year later.

The wings of the triptych, depicting *The Visitation*, *The Presentation in the Temple* and, when closed, the Guild's patron saint S. Christopher were not completed until 1613. The preparatory oil sketches for the wings (Princes Gate Collection) and their exteriors (Alte Pinakothek, Munich) were probably painted after Rubens received the commission.

Rubens had first confronted the subject of *The Descent from the Cross* in a drawing now in The Hermitage, Leningrad. Although the date of this drawing is uncertain, it obviously served Rubens as a point of departure when he came to tackle the complex composition in the oil sketch. The curved body of Christ, the back-turned figure of S. John standing on the right, Joseph of Arimathea balanced on the ladder to the left, the kneeling figures of the Magdalen and Mary Cleophas and the distinctive figure of the man above the cross holding the shroud in his teeth are anticipated in the Leningrad drawing.

Both the drawing and the oil sketch bear a direct reference to a fresco painted in 1541 by Daniele da Volterra in S. Trinità dei Monti which Rubens would have surely known from his visits to Rome. In the drawing Rubens followed the Italian tradition, used in the fresco, of showing the Virgin swooning and supported by another figure. In the oil sketch and the altarpiece that followed it, Rubens gave the Virgin a more active role and she reaches up, with a deeply poignant gesture, to receive the body of her son.

The oil sketch is more highly finished and coloured, more tightly executed and larger than the oil sketches for the wings and, indeed, the majority of Rubens' oil sketches. Its excellent state of preservation stands testimony to the great skill, craftsmanship and care which Rubens brought to its execution. The discrepancies in the level of finish can be attributed, at least partially, to the important purpose the oil sketch for the central panel served in securing the commission. The painting techniques are entirely consistent with those Rubens reserved for his oil sketches thus dismissing suggestions that it may be a copy by Rubens after the altarpiece.   N.T.

Sir Peter Paul Rubens (1577–1640)

The Family of Jan Brueghel the Elder c.1613–15

Oil on panel, 124.5 × 94.6
Princes Gate Collection

The Antwerp painter Jan Brueghel (1568–1625) is portrayed here with his wife Catharina van Marienberg and their two eldest children, Peter (b.1608) and Elizabeth (b.1609). A son of the famous Pieter Bruegel the Elder, Jan specialised in detailed cabinet paintings. He was a close friend of Rubens, with whom he collaborated on many works, and who acted as his secretary in his correspondence with his Italian patron, Cardinal Borromeo.

The portrait is remarkable for its intimacy and informality. With three pairs of eyes looking out of the picture, the viewer's attention is directly engaged by the sitters. Catharina's central position in the composition, which is analogous to that of the Virgin in a painting of the Holy Family, expresses her central rôle in the family as mother and wife. The impression of a closely-knit family unit is conveyed largely through the interplay of arms and hands, particularly in their convergence on Catharina's lap. While Elizabeth gazes lovingly up at her mother, whose example, it is implied, she will aspire to follow, Peter's hand directs attention to her bracelet (one of a pair), probably a betrothal gift. Rubens' own wife Isabella Brant wears a similar pair in their marriage portrait in Munich.

No trappings of Jan Brueghel's profession appear. The couple are portrayed as respectable Antwerp burghers, their restrained but rich dress contrasting with the fashionable clothes sported by their children, Peter amusingly adopting a courtier's pose. Elizabeth's expensive coral necklace is of a type believed to protect children against evil. The portrait was painted c.1613–15.

While it is possible that the figure of Jan Brueghel was introduced only at a late stage in the evolution of the picture (there is an early copy with this figure missing), there is little doubt that it was intended to include him somewhere in the project, perhaps in the more traditional form of a pendant portrait. Rubens certainly integrated him convincingly into the spirit of the present composition, embracing as he does his whole family with his outstretched arm. An allusion to the idea of conjugal and family love as the source of an artist's inspiration (a theme discernible in contemporary Northern Netherlandish portraiture) may have been intended here. The contrast between the tighter execution and blander lighting of Catharina and the livelier treatment of Jan is explicable as a visual means of differentiating their characters, a concern also evinced by the choice of a different type of ruff for each member of the family.

That this painting of one leading Antwerp artist by another passed by marriage into the possession of a third (David Teniers II) vividly reflects the close ties between the artistic community in the city.   J.W. & A.W.-L.

Sir Peter Paul Rubens (1577–1640)

The Daughters of Cecrops discovering Erichthonius c.1615

Oil on panel, 39.9 × 48.8
Princes Gate Collection

This is a sketch for the large painting in the Liechtenstein collection, Vaduz, from which it differs in some important details. The Liechtenstein painting is usually dated c.1615–17, and this sketch was probably done in about 1615.

Rubens has used the story of Erichthonius as told by Ovid in the *Metamorphoses* (II, 553–63), which is less tragic in its outcome than the version of the myth first related in Euripides' *Ion*, and repeated with variations by later authors. Erichthonius was accidentally conceived by Vulcan while attempting to ravish Minerva; Mother Earth (Gaea or Ge), who here appears transformed as a fountain statue of Diana of Ephesus (Artemis Ephesia), gave birth to him in the form of a half-serpent. Minerva entrusted the little monster in a sealed basket to Herse, Aglauros, and Pandrosus, the three daughters of King Cecrops of Attica. Rubens has chosen the moment when Aglauros disobeys Minerva's strict command, and opens the basket. (In some versions of the story, the child is normal but is found with a serpent lying beside him.) In the Euripidean story, this disobedience results in the suicide of the horrified sisters; but Ovid relates that the act was seen by a crow who tittle-tattled the story to Minerva and was punished for this. Julius Held has further elucidated the meaning of both the Vaduz and London pictures by observing that Herse, described as the most beautiful of the sisters, is later wooed by Mercury, while Aglauros is punished for her continued display of pride.

In the London sketch, the figure standing on the left is Herse, and the presence of a peacock may be an indirect reference to Juno, whose attribute it is, and thus to the future marriage of Herse and Mercury, over which Juno presided. Rubens returned to the subject in the 1630s; it may also be interpreted as a celebration of nature and fecundity. The shadowy figure to the right of Herse in this sketch, is transformed in the Vaduz picture to a striking Sybil-like figure of an old woman, who is prophetic of the Future. The Past is also symbolised by the stone figure of Mother Earth/Diana of Ephesus, on the right of the picture.

This sketch is unfinished, but it enables us to see how Rubens exploits the use of grey underpaint washed over with a thin brownish tint which produces the translucent half-tones, especially in parts of the flesh painting, that give such sparkling vivacity to his work.   D.F.

Sir Peter Paul Rubens (1577–1640)

The Death of Achilles early 1630s

Oil on panel, 107 × 108
Princes Gate Collection

The Death of Achilles is the final episode in a series of eight scenes from the life of the Greek hero, which served as designs for a cycle of tapestries. In the temple of Apollo at Thymbra, near Troy, where he was about to marry the princess Polyxena, Achilles falls victim to Trojan treachery. Guided by Apollo, the champion of the Trojan cause, Paris' arrow pierces Achilles' heel, his one vulnerable spot. The figure in lilac robes is probably the priest Calchas. Below the 'stage' on which the main drama takes place, a symbolic group echoes the central action: the mighty hero (eagle) is vanquished by the wily Paris (fox). Flanking the design are two sculpted herms of Venus (with Cupid) and Apollo (with the snake-like monster Python). In an amusing conceit, these deities appear to observe dispassionately the tragedy for which they between them were ultimately responsible. Above, a cartouche flanked by putti and swags completes the framing structure, which is a consistent, unifying feature of the series.

Nothing definite is known about the origins of the project, but circumstantial evidence strongly suggests that the designs were produced in the early 1630s, perhaps as a speculative venture, for (or in collaboration with) Rubens' father-in-law, Daniel Fourment, an Antwerp tapestry dealer. The present *modello* is a faithful enlargement of an oil sketch (Rotterdam), and would have served both as the pattern for the full scale cartoon from which the tapestry was woven, and as a contract painting, on the basis of which prospective clients might order a set of tapestries. Their high degree of finish would also have made such works saleable objects in their own right. Clarity of design and detail is typical of Rubens' *modelli* for projects like tapestries and engravings, the final execution of which was beyond his direct control.

The basic literary source for the life of Achilles is Homer's great epic, the *Iliad*. However, the demise of the hero is only hinted at by Homer, and Rubens drew here (as he did extensively in this series) on later, elaborated versions of the story. But while Renaissance commentators had interpreted Achilles' downfall in moralistic terms, as a consequence of his 'lustful love' for Polyxena, Rubens rather stresses the drama and pathos of the event. Indeed, the expression and pose of the dying Achilles evoke the famous Classical sculptures of Laocöon (Vatican) and the Dying Alexander (Uffizi), which in Rubens' time were regarded as the supreme embodiment of pathos. Moreover, Laocöon had been a priest of the very temple of Apollo where the present scene takes place. The introduction of these associations is characteristic of Rubens' harnessing of the Antique to enrich his own art.

There was no precedent for such a comprehensive treatment of the life of Achilles, and Rubens with his profound knowledge of Antiquity must surely have relished the opportunity to display his erudition and powers of invention.

The Wrath of Achilles, also in the Princes Gate Collection, is part of the same series.

A.W.-L.

Sir Peter Paul Rubens (1577–1640)

Landscape by Moonlight c.1635–40

Oil on panel, 64 × 90
Princes Gate Collection

In 1635 Rubens bought the country estate of Het Steen, to which he retreated as often as possible during the last years of his life, enjoying domestic felicity with his young second wife, Helena Fourment, and their growing family. There, too, he painted many of the landscapes which are an outstanding feature of his last decade, and in some of which appear the castle of Het Steen or surrounding landmarks. He took pleasure in recording impressions of different times of day, the effects of light in sunrise or sunset or, in this case, in moonlight.

The air of nocturnal solitude in this scene is unique among Rubens' paintings. He was perhaps originally inspired by moonlit settings of biblical scenes, especially by the magical *Flight into Egypt* by the German, Adam Elsheimer, whose small-scale works he had first admired in Rome early in the century. Here, for the first time, the moon presides over a scene without human figures. We know now, however, from scientific examination, that Rubens first created an inhabited landscape and achieved the finished effect only after a complicated and searching process of experiment. The original painting, not untypically with Rubens, was smaller. It contained, as well as the grazing horse, hastily sketched-in figures including a woman in a broad-brimmed hat holding a baby, who do not appear to represent the Holy Family, seated in the foreground beneath the central tree and warmed by a blazing fire. Subsequently, Rubens added a further panel of wood of 26cm to the right and a strip of 15cm along the top (the skilful joins are just visible), altered the original disposition of the trees and experimented with a number of other figures – possibly nymphs and satyrs – across the foreground of the right-hand addition. Finally, all the figures were painted out, the barn only serving as a reminder of man's presence.

The moon magically dominates now over nature, its light cast in different colours about the surrounding clouds, making a path across the water beneath, catching between tree-trunks the ripples of the stream flowing to the right, and of its tributary in the distance; it attempts to enter with short incursions the impenetrable gloom of the trees sketchily rendered on the right. Raised blobs of paint represent stars, some glittering through foliage or reflected in water. At the top is a shooting star.

By at least 1778 the *Landscape by Moonlight* had reached England. In that year Sir Joshua Reynolds, its first recorded owner, used it for demonstration in his 'Eighth Discourse' for the Royal Academy. This poetic and personal depiction of nature, novel in Rubens' time, was appreciated and admired by English artists from Gainsborough onwards, and we know that Constable died with his feet nearly touching 'a print of the beautiful moonlight by Rubens'. H.B.

Sir Anthony van Dyck (1599–1641)

Christ on the Cross c.1618–20

Oil on panel, 62.6 × 46.5
Lee Collection

Most of van Dyck's Crucifixions are painted as full-scale scenes with the three crosses and a crowd mourning at the base of Christ's cross. This picture, however, is a small devotional image reflecting the ideas of the Counter-Reformation contained in texts such as the *Spiritual Exercises* of S. Ignatius Loyola (1548):

> 'Speak with Him of how, being the Creator He then became man, and how possessing eternal life, He submitted to temporal death to die for our sins . . .'

Rubens was one of the first, c.1610, to depict Christ alive on the cross, alone, looking heavenward, receiving the Holy Spirit almost in a state of ecstasy, and at the moment of extreme suffering. Van Dyck, who assisted Rubens in his early years in Antwerp, followed his example in what became the most popular portrayal of Christ on the cross in the 17th century. Both artists also painted, although less frequently, Christ dead on the cross. It is the moment after expiring when we are shown a more human aspect. Darkness is all around, except for a glimmer from the moon hidden behind the cross, over the distant city. This italianate city is supposed to be Jerusalem on which Christ has turned his back. He is lit from an unknown source, illuminated against the gloomy sky to emphasise the contorted form of the dead body, as if it is set in relief.

The dead Christ is not idealised; blood trickles down the arms and from the feet. His head, bearded and crowned with thorns, is bent downwards and the halo is but a faint aura. Only a skull is left between the viewer and Christ, a reference to Golgotha, 'place of the skull'. The skull, traditionally thought to be Adam's, is an obvious reminder of death. Van Dyck treats the subject realistically but eschews the expressionist element of those earlier depictions which show a spout of blood from the gaping wound on the side – here barely visible. There is also a rather more unusual feature for here Christ is crucified with four nails, instead of by one nail only through the feet. Again, van Dyck is following Rubens' iconography who in turn must have been interpreting the writings of the great mystic S. Bridget of Sweden. In her *Revelations*, she says she had a vision of Christ in this way and particularly with one foot over the other.

The unusual painted monochrome border also signifies the Saviour's death for the Redemption of mankind and symbolises the Eucharist. Although on a separate piece fixed to the inner panel it is also believed to be by van Dyck. Such decoration was found on funerary monuments and in designs for triumphal arches or title pages. The demons, torches, cornucopia of fruit and flowers, the palm, and the sheaf of corn are all both secular and religious emblems but together represent a triumphal victory over death.

According to Bellori, van Dyck was befriended by Cardinal Guido Bentivoglio in Rome for whom he painted a crucifixion and it was, perhaps, this kind of small-scale picture. The treatment of our painting is less advanced and less robust than his other small crucifixes, which he may have painted in Italy between 1621–7. There is a telling quality, however, to the livid features of the face. This painting was probably executed about 1618–20 before van Dyck left Antwerp. It is not known for whom, and there is no inscription on the plaque in the painted frame.   T.J.

Claude Gellée, called Claude Lorrain (1600–82)

Landscape with an Imaginary View of Tivoli 1642

Copper, 21.6 × 25.8
Signed and dated, lower left: 'CLAVDIO (?) 1642'
Princes Gate Collection

This little painting is dated 1642, but the circumstances of its origin are not known. Claude made no reference to a patron or destination in his record of the work (no.67) in the *Liber Veritatis*; and the addition by a later hand of the name 'Robert Gayer', who was not born until c.1639, is misleading. This is thought to refer to Gayer's probable possession of a variant of the picture, which is now at Petworth and is almost certainly not by Claude. It seems likely that our painting was made as a memento for a traveller on his departure from Rome.

The date places the work at the end of Claude's earlier period when, in common with his painter friends from northern Europe, he had produced genre scenes: busy seaports which had occupied his imagination since an earlier stay in Naples, or landscapes with groups of musicians or dancers, or a herdsman with his cattle and goats. By the later 1640s there began to evolve what we think of as typical Claudian work: classical, biblical, or pastoral subjects quietly absorbed into the idyllic landscape of the Roman Campagna, where the light seems almost timeless yet is appropriate to the hour. In a distinction made by the late Anthony Blunt, what had been viewed with curiosity by earlier artists was now seen by Claude with the eyes of wonder.

In 1642, however, this was foreshadowed only in hints, and our painting is less sophisticated. The foreground is busy with its herdsman and his animals, and with the abundant plant life which would have delighted Elsheimer. Across a wooden bridge moves a horseman with his party – one of Claude's last figures in contemporary dress, soon to be succeeded by characters from mythology or the scriptures. Beyond the bridge the river is agitated by the falls, sheltered on the left by great trees, and overlooked on the right by the temple of the Sybil, by the just visible villa of Maecenas and a Romanesque church tower: a cluster of buildings doing poetic duty for Tivoli itself. The river winds towards the horizon where the dome of S. Peter's reminds us, as it would have reminded Claude's patron, of the not-so-distant Eternal City. Meanwhile, the early evening sun edges the clouds and the woodwork of the bridge with bright touches of gold, reserving for the distance a more subdued, serener light.

This little work is painted on copper – a support which Claude used on some 15 or so occasions but which gradually lost its popularity during his lifetime.

R.H.

Sir Peter Lely (1618–80)

The Concert ('Lely and his Family') late 1640s

Oil on canvas, 122.9 × 234.5
Lee Collection

Sir Peter Lely was the son of a Dutch army captain, and although he was born at Soest, Westphalia, he returned to Holland where he trained under Peter de Grebber at Haarlem. He became a Master in the Haarlem Guild in 1637. His family name was van der Faes, and the nickname by which he became known was derived from one of the houses, 'In de Lely', owned by his family in The Hague. Nothing is known of his work before he came to London, where he most probably arrived in 1643. His first certain portraits date from 1647, when he was patronised by the Earl of Northumberland, who introduced him to other noblemen.

During the Commonwealth and Protectorate, Lely painted mythological and historical pieces, as well as portraits, including one of Oliver Cromwell. His large personal fortune was established during the 1650s and he began to collect old master paintings and drawings on a considerable scale, including works by van Dyck sold from Charles I's collection. The portraits of this period are often austere in mood, although he could achieve a more playfully baroque style in his portrait groups and 'fancy conversation pieces', of which *The Concert* is one. These belong either to the late 1640s or, less likely, to 1658–9, after Lely's return from a prolonged visit to Holland. Although *The Concert* has been called 'An Idyll', and, at least as early as 1763, 'Lely and his Family', there is no foundation for this traditional identification. The seated musician may, however, be a self-portrait.

Painted with a vibrant touch in clear, fresh colours, this enchanting group shows seven figures, including two young children and a young woman gathered round the figure of a casually dressed man who plays a bass-violin (five-stringed cello). One child plays a flute and his two companions sing from a score to the accompaniment of the two instrumentalists. The half-draped female nude, also holding a sheet of music, her back half-turned to the bass-player, acts as a pivotal figure in the composition, linking the right-hand group of elegantly attired women and their dog, with the musicians on the left. A rich, plum-coloured expanse of silken material hangs down on the right like a theatrical backdrop, which half-envelops the woman standing by her companion who is seated on a throne. On the left, beyond the rocky outcrop, we catch a glimpse of distant landscape and ruins. It is as if we have surprised a discreetly 'bohemian' picnic party in some idealised sylvan glade. The painting looks back in colour and mood to the *fêtes champêtres* of 16th-century Venetian art and amusingly anticipates Manet's *Déjeuner sur l'herbe*. The courtly flavour of the Lely echoes the poetry of his friend, the cavalier, Richard Lovelace, and reflects Lely's own love of music. Some of the foreground drapery and other details are unfinished.

The meaning of this picture is obscure, but Oliver Millar has suggested that it represents the familiar allegory of Music in the service of Love and Beauty.

D.F.

Giovanni Battista Tiepolo (1696–1770)

Allegory of the Power of Eloquence c.1725

Oil on canvas, 46.5 × 67.5; within shaped border
Princes Gate Collection

This is a *modello* for Tiepolo's first surviving ceiling fresco decoration for the main salone on the second floor of the Palazzo Sandi at Venice, in the parish of S. Angelo, near the Grand Canal. The Sandi family had been ennobled in 1685, and were associated with the profession of law. The allegorical subject chosen of the Power of Eloquence may be an allusion to the Sandi family's legal distinction, but as Michael Levey points out in his monograph on the artist (1986), the triumph of mind over matter, of verbal cunning over brute force, has been extended to the power of sound, not only through words but through music. Minerva and Mercury occupy the centre of the stage as the deities of Wisdom and Eloquence.

The subsidiary themes which occupy the four sides of the ceiling which still survives in the Palazzo Sandi, appear in this preliminary sketch, but undergo important changes in the final scheme as the artist tightens up the composition so as to link more closely the five constituent elements, and to heighten the overall dramatic effect. Painted on a red ground, the *modello* may lack the sparkle and luminosity of the final fresco, but gives us an interesting insight into Tiepolo's fast-developing creative genius.

The four supporting heroic themes are, clockwise from the bottom: Amphion, by the power of music, causing the walls of Thebes to build themselves; Orpheus leading Eurydice past Cerberus; Hercules 'Gallicus' enchains people by the power of speech; and Bellerophon on his winged horse, Pegasus, slays the Chimera. The most important group is of Amphion surrounded by the amazed Thebans, and it was this scene which would be the first to confront the spectator as he entered the room and looked up at the ceiling. But Tiepolo has altered the positions of the Bellerophon and Orpheus groups (right and left, respectively, in the *modello*) on the finished ceiling, by placing Bellerophon on the left side and substituting Hercules in his place. Orpheus is moved to the top of the composition, thereby strengthening the link between the two 'musical' elements, and placing Bellerophon and Hercules in counterpoint. Tiepolo also more satisfactorily integrates Minerva and Mercury into the final composition, by making them larger and creating around them two almost interlocking whirlpools of cloud, which, in turn, act as a foil to a brilliantly lit golden empyrean that is only tentatively indicated in this preliminary *modello*. The Palazzo Sandi frescoes were almost certainly finished by 1726, for in the June of that year Tiepolo was commissioned to paint decorations in a chapel at the Duomo in Udine.

D.F.

Giovanni Battista Tiepolo (1696–1770)

The Immaculate Conception 1769

Oil on canvas, 63.5 × 38.5; within a shaped border,
internal measurement, 56 × 30
Princes Gate Collection

This *modello* is for one of the seven altarpieces commissioned by Charles III of Spain from Tiepolo in March 1767, which were destined for S. Pascual Baylon, the monastery church of the Alcantarine Discalced Franciscans at Aranjuez, south of Madrid, built by Francesco Sabatini between 1765–70. Five of the *modelli*, including this one, have survived and are in the Princes Gate Collection. The *modelli* were finished by early August 1767, and Tiepolo was authorized to proceed with the main commission a month later. Tiepolo completed the commission, aided by his son Domenico, by August 1769, but did not live to see them placed in position in the church for which they were intended. He died three weeks after his 74th birthday on 27 March 1770. Joaquin de Eleta, Charles III's confessor, was the delegate for this commission and his hostility to Tiepolo, and the rivalry of Anton Raphael Mengs, may have been responsible for the dismantling of six of the altarpieces (one, *S. Charles Borromeo*, was never placed in the church) and their subsequent dispersal. Tiepolo's paintings were replaced in the 1770s with altarpieces by Maella, Mengs, and Francisco Bayeu (Goya's brother-in-law), who once owned the five Tiepolo *modelli*.

The *Immaculate Conception* altarpiece was sited in the north transept of S. Pascual, and is now in the Prado Museum, Madrid. The subject was not a new one in Tiepolo's work, and the Franciscans were among the chief protagonists of the dogma of the Immaculate Conception, which, although it had a long history of observance, only received its final definition and acceptance in a Papal Bull of 1854. There are significant changes between the composition as it appears in the *modello* and in its final state, and these may be due to second thoughts by the artist, or may have been made in response to his patron's criticisms. We know that on completion of the commission, he had written to the King's secretary, Miguel de Muzquiz, to express his willingness to alter anything in the finished works which did not please. Some alterations were made to the other altarpieces. The finished altarpiece is 279 × 152 cm, and Tiepolo has simplified the composition by omitting the large supporting angel on the right and the two cherubs in the sky on the left. The position of the serpent, symbolical of Original Sin, has been reversed; the cherub bearing a stem of lilies, symbol of purity, is shown in a pose of humble veneration rather than, as in the *modello*, joyously holding up the lilies in adoration. The Dove of the Holy Trinity has also been given greater prominence, and the composition made more compact.

Tiepolo had originally intended the altarpiece to have a rectangular format with a stepped top, and he indicated the intended shapes of each of the altarpieces in the *modelli*. This attention to detail is characteristic of the care he took over this major commission. It has to be said, however, that the finished version of the *Immaculate Conception* lacks the exuberant vitality and supreme self-confidence so manifest in this brilliantly executed preliminary study.   D.F.

George Romney (1734–1802)

Georgiana, Lady Greville c.1771–72

Oil on canvas, 76.1 × 63.5
Lee Collection

George Romney was the son of a Lancashire cabinet-maker and was apprenticed to an itinerant portrait painter, Christopher Steele, from 1755–7, before setting up on his own in Kendal. He moved to London in 1762 and although he tried his hand at history painting, soon established himself as a portrait painter. He had skill enough to capture a good superficial likeness and responded to youth and good looks; his portraits lack the *gravitas* of Reynolds or the rococo brilliance of Gainsborough, nor was he stirred to produce portraits of great personal insight into the character of his sitters. Of nervous and introspective disposition, he took little interest in society at large nor did he participate in the affairs of his own profession and rarely exhibited his work. Apart from a visit to Paris in 1764, and two years spent in Italy (1773–5), he remained in London until, in 1798, he retired a sick man to Kendal.

It might be thought that such an unsociable man would be quite unsuited to become a fashionable portrait painter, but as Ellis Waterhouse observed, it was precisely these qualities of detachment and artistic neutrality which were his strengths. For he was able to 'bring forward all those neutral qualities which are valued by Society – health, youth, good looks, an air of breeding, or at least of the tone of the highest ranks of the social scale.' His prices were also always lower than those of either Reynolds or Gainsborough.

This portrait of Georgiana, Lady Greville, painted in either 1771 or 1772, just before Romney's Italian journey, epitomises both the positive and negative aspects of his art. Lady Greville is shown half-length, her body slightly turned to the spectator's left, her head tilted in contraposto to the right. Her gloved hands clasp her folded arms and form a secondary focal point to the triangle of the head and body. She wears a fashionable lace headdress enlivened by pink bows, her dress is hidden under a black, lace-trimmed shawl. She is silhouetted against a nondescript blue background which might suggest the open sky yet is palpably a studio backdrop. The composition is simple yet elegant, the modelling crisp but slightly papery.

Georgiana Peachey (1752–72) was the only daughter of Sir James Peachey, later Lord Selsey; on 1 April 1771 she married George, then known as Lord Greville, who later became 2nd Earl of Warwick. Lady Greville died on her first wedding anniversary, and never became Countess of Warwick.   D.F.

Thomas Gainsborough (1727–88)

Mrs Thomas Gainsborough, née Margaret Burr c.1778

Oil on canvas, 76.8 × 64.1
Samuel Courtauld Collection

Thomas Gainsborough's painting of his wife Margaret (1728–98), whom he married in 1746, departs in certain significant ways from his commissioned female portraits. While he frequently exploited the bust-length format to enhance the fiction of an intimate encounter between sitter and spectator, the requirements of 'modesty' as a social norm for women demanded that such intimacy be kept at a distance. Thus most comparable Gainsborough portraits either show their subjects turned (or at least looking) slightly away from the viewer, or – and more commonly – they place the sitter within an illusionistic painted oval which separates her from the viewer. Here, however, the painter has arranged his wife's hands, head and drapery to enact the part of that feigned oval, and in so doing has given her presence an aura of unusual immediacy which is reinforced by the frontality of her gaze. Ladies of quality were not meant to present themselves with such directness to their portraitists, or to the outside world in general; for the 18th-century Englishwoman, this sort of look was to be reserved exclusively for her husband. 'I would have the husband firmly persuaded', one writer advised married women in 1756, 'that his bride has a great deal of tenderness in her heart; but would have no room for him to entertain a thought that she has so much in her composition as to make her able to bestow the least portion of it on any other than himself.' In the Courtauld picture, Margaret Gainsborough seems perfectly designed to play this rôle: her exposure of tenderness is both limited and temporary, a moment of conjugal intimacy that only serves to dramatise a commitment to modesty which is signified by the enclosing mantle and the concealing bows. Though this private image (a 50th birthday present?) may suggest Gainsborough's affection for his wife, it nonetheless asserts a husband's power through a display of pictorial 'mastery'.

D.H.S.

This was probably the first painting Samuel Courtauld bought in his collecting career, which began in 1921, and had once belonged to his wife's family. The delicate femininity of this portrait bears comparison with another of his early purchases, Renoir's *La Loge*, which was one of his favourite pictures.

D.F.

Edouard Manet (1832–83)

Le Déjeuner sur l'herbe c.1863?

Oil on canvas, 89.5 × 116.5
Signed, lower left: 'Manet'
Samuel Courtauld Collection

This is a smaller version of the famous *Déjeuner sur l'herbe* (Musée d'Orsay, Paris), which was rejected by the Salon jury in 1863 and exhibited as *Le Bain* at the Salon des Refusés of 1863. The models in the large picture have been identified as Victorine Meurent (a professional model), either Gustave or Eugène Manet (brothers of the painter) and Ferdinand Leenhoff, a Dutch sculptor, whose sister Manet married in 1863. The picture caused much controversy when it was exhibited at the Salon des Refusés, and critics and historians still dispute the artist's intentions. Antonin Proust records Manet's ambition to rework the theme of the Giorgione *Concert champêtre* in the Louvre in a more luminous, outdoor ambience; but the final painting was undoubtedly executed in the studio, apparently based on studies made on the Ile Saint-Ouen, on the Seine on the northern outskirts of Paris. There is another link with Renaissance painting: the poses of the three main figures are directly based on a group of nymphs and river gods from the right side of an engraving by Marcantonio Raimondi after Raphael's lost *Judgment of Paris*. Manet was also aware of the *fêtes galantes* of French 18th-century painters such as Watteau, and of recent popular romantic prints by artists such as Devéria and Morlon, which, in a more 'popular' medium, lent a more overtly erotic content to Watteau-like themes.

The large painting puzzled contemporary critics for several reasons. The juxtaposition of a naked woman with men in modern dress was regarded as indecent; the woman's body was seen as ugly – not conforming to academic canons of beauty – and the men's clothing, particularly the smoking-cap of the figure on the right, led critics to identify them as students; the handling of the picture did not differentiate sufficiently figures from background, both being treated in broad, vigorous touches of paint. The type of subject was unclear: its very large scale (about 7 by 9 feet) led them to expect a picture with a significant subject; its naked figure led them to expect nymphs and naiads; and the picnic scene recalled the *fête champêtre*. However, the painting itself conformed to none of these types, but rather deliberately flouted the conventions of each; in a sense it was a parody of the tenets of contemporary academic 'high' art, enshrining a scene from contemporary bohemian life in the language, and on the scale, of history painting. Moreover, the gaze of the naked woman, looking away from her companions and directly at the viewer, made it impossible to conceive of the scene taking place in some sylvan glade of the imagination.

The status of the Courtauld version has been debated, was it a preparatory sketch, or a replica made after the large version, from which it differs in a number of details? X-ray examination of both canvases has clarified matters. The Courtauld picture shows no significant changes during its execution; by contrast, the large version was very extensively changed, and originally included an open vista with small trees in its left background, instead of the trunk and foliage which now frame it. It thus seems virtually certain that the Courtauld version is a replica, made after the big one was completed, and refining its arrangement in minor ways. Its first owner was Manet's friend the Commandant Lejosne; and it seems likely that because he was unable to house the big painting, he asked the artist to make a reduced version. We cannot be sure when this was done; indeed, the breadth and simplicity of handling in the Courtauld picture suggests that it was executed a few years after the large version.   J.H.

Edouard Manet (1832–83)

A Bar at the Folies-Bergère 1881–2

Oil on canvas, 96 × 130
Signed on wine bottle label, lower left: 'Manet/1882'
Samuel Courtauld Collection

A Bar at the Folies-Bergère was Manet's last major completed painting, exhibited at the Paris Salon in 1882, a year before his death. It shows the interior of one of the most fashionable café-concerts in Paris, and Manet made rapid preparatory sketches in the Folies-Bergère itself; however, the final painting (and also, it seems, the oil sketch for it) was executed in Manet's studio, using one of the barmaids, by the name of Suzon, who worked in the Folies-Bergère as a model. Georges Jeanniot visited Manet's studio in January 1882 and described him at work on the canvas, with the model posed behind a table laden with bottles and foodstuffs: 'Although he worked from the model, he did not copy nature at all closely; I noted his masterly simplifications. . . . Everything was abbreviated; the tones were made lighter, the colours brighter; the values were more closely related to each other, the tones more contrasting.' Manet insisted that 'concision in art was a necessity'.

In the preliminary oil sketch (Stedelijk Museum, Amsterdam), the barmaid's head is half turned towards the right, with her reflection in the mirror behind the bar in a readily intelligible position, just to the right of the figure, while the reflection of her customer appears near the right edge of the composition, at a lower level; he wears a bowler hat and carries a cane. In the final version, the barmaid is separated far too far from her reflection; the customer is shown in the reflection close to the barmaid, whereas in fact the spectator is placed at some distance from the image that looks out of the picture; and the placing of the bottles in the reflection does not correspond to their position on the bar in the foreground – they are near the 'wrong' edge of the bar. X-ray photographs of the final painting show that initially its forms were close to those in the sketch, and thus were logically coherent; substantial changes were made during the execution of the picture, most notably the moving of the reflection of the barmaid to the right (this took place in two stages), and the replacement of the customer with the bowler hat and cane (as in the sketch) by the man in the top right. Thus the discrepancies between the principal image and the reflections in the final version were introduced absolutely deliberately, and evolved as Manet worked up the picture. The result is that the barmaid is presented to the viewer very directly, as an iconic centre of the composition; but a disturbing dislocation is created, between the apparent directness of her encounter with the man seen in the mirror, and her seeming distance and abstractedness as she faces the viewer. The figures seen in the mirror to the left of the barmaid, are seated in the circle seats on the opposite side of the auditorium; the *demi-mondaine* Méry Laurent posed for the woman in a white dress with yellow gloves, the young actress Jeanne Demarsy for the figure immediately behind her, in a box. Throughout his career Manet had avoided compositions which showed easily legible relationships between figures and presented clear-cut narratives, in favour of subjects where the status of the figures remained unclear, and groupings which defied the viewer's attempts to interpret them. This was in part a rejection of the conventions of the fashionable genre painting of the day, but also an attempt to convey a more vivid sense of actuality, in which relationships between people are rarely so clear-cut and unambiguous as they had traditionally been depicted in painting.

The status of the barmaids at the Folies-Bergère was ambivalent: they were primarily there to serve drinks, but they were also potentially available to their clients themselves; they might themselves become commodities, like the bottles on the bar. Manet's picture, with its wilful distortion of perceived experience, seems designed to enshrine this uncertainty. This is enhanced by the way in which it is painted, for the bottles and fruit bowl on the bar are treated with great richness and finesse while the figure of the barmaid is more broadly and simply treated. Manet's pictorial world was a challenge to social as well as artistic values. J.H.

Honoré Daumier (1808–79)

Don Quixote and Sancho Panza

Oil on canvas, 100 × 81
Samuel Courtauld Collection

Between 1848 and the early 1870s Daumier produced 29 paintings and over 40 drawings from Cervantes' *Don Quixote*. These works focus on three main motifs: Don Quixote or Sancho Panza resting beneath a tree, portrait studies of Don Quixote, and, most frequently, the dreaming knight and his prosaic squire riding forth to engage in chivalric adventures. Despite his reputation as a caricaturist, and the potential for satiric comedy in Cervantes' characters, Daumier does not treat them as subjects of grotesque humour, but concentrates on interpreting the idealistic, even fanatic aspiration of the hero.

Daumier's earliest biographer, Arsène Alexandre, recognised an empathy of spirit between Daumier and his favourite literary characters. This characterisation suggests that Don Quixote, as the archetypal visionary, is identifiable with the artist himself and that as man and artist Daumier 'had the soul of Don Quixote in the body of Sancho Panza'.

French artists had previously chosen *Don Quixote* subjects during the 17th and 18th centuries, and amongst Daumier's contemporaries Cervantes' novel attracted artists such as Delacroix, Daubigny, Corot and Doré. But Daumier's sense of identification between artist and subject is most complete. When seen through Daumier's romantic imagination the figure of the idealistic knight, striving for the unachievable dream, is given an air of tragic nobility, only heightened by its spiritual and physical contrast with the more earth-bound and earthy Sancho.

In most of Daumier's depictions of the ill-assorted pair, mounted on their varied steeds (Don Quixote on his gaunt Rocinante and Sancho Panza on the squat-shaped ass, Dapple), the servant is seen following in the wake of his master, a protective figure shadowing the knight whose visionary idealism leads so often to disasters from which Sancho's peasant common sense and realism must rescue him. Uniquely, however, in this painting, which is Daumier's largest treatment of the theme, the two contrasting characters are shown in equilibrium. Although undated, it is probably one of Daumier's last realisations of this very personal theme, before increasing blindness caused him to cease painting in 1873. Here we see the figures of Don Quixote and Sancho Panza on a grandiose and equal scale, riding side by side, as if reconciliation and balance, rather than antithesis and contrast, can be achieved between the polarities of romantic aspiration and earthy realism. While the elongated lines of Don Quixote and Rocinante suggest an upwards tension the more rotund forms of Sancho Panza and Dapple provide a counterweight tugging the dreamer knight back towards the earth and the worldly.   C.G.

Camille Pissarro (1830–1903)

Lordship Lane Station, Dulwich 1871

Oil on canvas, 44.5 × 72.5
Signed, lower right: 'C. Pissarro 1871'
Samuel Courtauld Collection

Pissarro painted this picture while living in London as a refugee from the Franco-Prussian war in 1870–1. Formerly known as *Penge Station, Upper Norwood*, its correct location has recently been identified as Lordship Lane Station (now demolished) on the old Crystal Palace (High Level) Railway, seen from the footbridge across the cutting to the south of the station. The line was opened in 1865 to cater for the crowds coming to the Crystal Palace, very popular as a recreation and exhibition centre since its reconstruction in this South London suburb in 1852–4. Thus the scene shows a modern landscape in the making, with the rows of new houses on either side of the station framed by still-undeveloped open land. Many of Pissarro's canvases painted while he was living in nearby Norwood focus on the burgeoning suburban developments around the Crystal Palace, and some show the palace itself.

Here the chosen subject is deliberately anti-picturesque, with the wide, scrubby slopes and drab fences framing the central motif of tracks and train. Several of the Impressionist group painted railway trains, including Manet and Monet, but this canvas seems to be the first occasion on which one of them made a train into his central motif. It may echo Turner's famous *Rain, Steam and Speed*, which Pissarro saw in the National Gallery in London, but, in place of Turner's lavish atmospherics, Pissarro adopted a far more detached view, closer in its treatment to contemporary topographical prints of the new railway landscape. The signal, silhouetted against the sky in the exact centre of the picture, can be seen as an utterly secularised equivalent of a crucifix – an overt rejection of traditional elevated subject matter, in the search for the truly contemporary.

The picture is quite subdued in colour; the effect of an overcast day is evoked by varied greens and soft red-browns, with the white of the smoke and the clear black of the engine as a central focus. This comparatively tonal treatment, with nuances of a restricted range of colour, is in marked contrast to the lavish colour which, soon afterwards, Monet began to adopt in sunlit scenes, and to the multicoloured interplay of touches which Pissarro himself later adopted. The brushwork is softly variegated to suggest the different textures in the scene; there is no dominant rhythm to the touch, which stresses the diversity of the elements which went to make up this characteristically modern landscape.

X-ray and infra-red photographs show that there was originally a figure, perhaps holding a scythe, on the bank to the right of the tracks, above the point on the bottom edge of the picture where the grass meets the ballast of the track. The position of the arms was altered before the figure was painted out altogether.

J.H.

76

Edgar Degas (1839–1917)

Two Dancers on the Stage 1874

Oil on canvas, 61.5 × 46
Signed, lower left: 'Degas'
Samuel Courtauld Collection

This composition is closely related to a group of three compositions with many figures, which show dancers rehearsing on a clearly defined stage, with other waiting dancers and the ballet master (two in the Metropolitan Museum of Art, New York, one in the Musée d'Orsay, Paris). Here, though, Degas concentrated on the two figures, with stage-flats beyond them which seem to suggest foliage, but gives no indication of whether we are watching a performance or a rehearsal, or any clue about the action under way. Our attention is focused on their poses, as seen from the unexpected angle of a box virtually above the edge of the stage. The viewer's attempt to see this as a coherent, framed grouping is undermined by the appearance of the edge of a third dancer, her figure cut by the frame, at the far left, set back on the stage, whose presence challenges any attempt to understand the gestures of the other two: they are in standard ballet positions, one *sur les pointes*, the other in fourth position with her arms in *demi-seconde*, but this is all we are told.

This canvas is unusually highly finished for Degas, and was put on exhibition and sold soon after its completion; contemporary reviews show that it was exhibited in London in November 1874 in the Ninth Exhibition of the Society of French Artists, organised by the Parisian dealer Paul Durand-Ruel, and it was bought at this show by the pioneering Degas collector, Captain Henry Hill of Brighton; it was the first painting by Degas that he bought.

The stage-flats in *Two Dancers on the Stage* are treated in free dabs of colour, but the figures are modelled with comparative delicacy. The overall colour scheme is quite subdued, with vivid points of pink, yellow and green on the figures' shoes, flowers, bodices and head-dresses. The generally simple paint surfaces and muted tonality are in marked contrast to the broken touch and vivid colour characteristic of the landscapists in the Impressionist group.

The canvas is the product of extensive preparatory work, and Degas made a number of alterations to the composition during its execution: the dancer cut off at the left was originally a little larger and about half an inch further to the right; and there are changes in the placing of the feet and legs of the two main dancers.

On occasions Degas painted actual ballet performances, but more often he showed the dancers rehearsing, or left it ambiguous what exactly they were doing, as here. The ballet, with its precision of movements, fascinated him, but he always presented it in ways which revealed its artificiality, by including other extraneous elements – figures who do not watch the dancers, waiting dancers scratching themselves, or dancers who play no part in the main action, like the figure on the left here. His interest in this theme is also part of his attempt in the 1870s to study the visible world from many angles which had not been sanctioned in previous art, but which seemed to him characteristic of the ways in which everyday life appeared in the modern city.   J.H.

Claude Monet (1840–1926)

Autumn effect at Argenteuil 1873

Oil on canvas, 55 × 74.5
Signed, lower right: 'Claude Monet/73'
Samuel Courtauld Collection

The town of Argenteuil is in the background, seen looking upstream along an arm of the river Seine, with the Ile Marante on the left; the blue stripe running across below the buildings represents the main channel of the river, flowing from right to left. The picture corresponds closely to Frederick Wedmore's description of a canvas shown at Dowdeswell's Gallery in London in 1883: '. . . palpitating light and golden hue. The whole one side of the canvas is filled with flame-coloured autumn trees which throw their bright reflection of a rosier flame-colour upon a broad river-water otherwise turquoise and coral.'

Of all Monet's paintings of the early 1870s, this is the one in which he most completely abandoned traditional methods of chiaroscuro modelling, by gradations from dark to light tones, in favour of a composition based on clear colours, which are used to model form and evoke space. The picture is dominated by the bold contrast between orange and blue, but the glowing bank of autumnal trees is built up from constantly varied warm hues – pinks and yellows as well as oranges; on the right, soft clear blues indicate the shadows in the trees, and the blues on the far buildings, together with the diminishing scale of the brushstrokes in the water, suggest recession into atmospheric space. The paint surface is densely worked in parts – almost as if encrusted on the trees on the left. Late in the execution of the picture, Monet scraped away some of this paint in long crisp strokes, probably made with the handle of a brush; these are most visible on the right tree, but also appear in the foliage on the left. Presumably they are the result of Monet's dissatisfaction with the density of the paint layers, but such scraping is extremely unusual in his work.

As often in his landscapes, Monet avoided a direct perspectival lead into the pictorial space, in favour of an open-fronted view across water, so that the viewer is invited to contemplate the spectacle rather than enter into the space in the imagination. At this period Argenteuil was rapidly expanding, both as an industrial town and as a centre for recreational sailing. Often Monet presented the modern facets of the place, but here it appears as if timeless, a few houses presided over by a church spire, framed by the splendour of the sunlit trees.   J.H.

Pierre-Auguste Renoir (1841–1919)

La Loge 1874

Oil on canvas, 80 × 63.5
Signed, lower left: 'A. Renoir 74'
Samuel Courtauld Collection

The artist's brother Edmond and a model, Nini (otherwise known as *Gueule-de-Raie* or 'fish-face'), from Montmartre posed for this painting, which was one of Renoir's prime exhibits at the first group exhibition of the Impressionists in Paris in 1874; the dealer Durand-Ruel then exhibited it in London, but did not buy it, and Renoir sold it in 1875 to another, less ambitious dealer, *père* Martin, for 425 francs – money which Renoir desperately needed in order to pay the rent.

It was at the first group exhibition in Paris in 1874 that the comments of critics about Monet's *Impression, Sunrise* (Musée Marmottan, Paris) led to the group being christened 'Impressionists'. However, Renoir's *La Loge* is very different from Monet's rapid sketch.

Yet the technique of *La Loge* is very fluent; forms are delicately and softly brushed without crisp contours, and the execution of the model's bodice and the flowers on it is a particularly virtuoso display. Her face, though, is executed more minutely, its modelling more fully suggested, which makes it the unequivocal focus of the composition. The model's gown, with its bold stripes, gives the composition a strong black and white underpinning; actual black paint is used here, though often mixed with blue to suggest the play of light and shade across it. Around its strong pattern, richly varied nuances of blues, greens and yellow recur in the white materials, set against the soft warm hues of her flesh and the pinks and reds in the flowers on her bodice and hair.

The subject of the theatre box was a favoured one among painters of modern Parisian life during the 1870s. In *La Loge* Renoir makes a play on the contrast between the poses of the two figures: the woman looks out with a half smile on her face and her opera glasses beside her, in her hand, as if to receive the gaze of other members of the audience, while her male companion looks through his opera glasses out from the box and upwards, and thus implicitly at another box, not down at the stage. The caricaturist Gavarni had already explored the same idea in a well-known drawing titled *A Lioness in Her Box*, but with the added satirical point that his woman, seated in the confident expectation of the admiration of her onlookers, is clearly ageing and past her prime, while her male companion peers through his binoculars with evident excitement. Renoir defused this, by presenting his model as young and pretty, seated to receive the gaze of her (male) viewers, while her companion is relegated to the half shadow behind her. In his treatment of his model, Renoir left her exact social and sexual status ambiguous; one of the reviewers of the first group exhibition (where the canvas was well received) described her as a typical *cocotte*, and another as 'a figure from the world of elegance'. Such an elision of the signs of difference was very characteristic of Renoir; unlike Manet, he never painted images which suggested any social uncertainty or division, but, in his paintings of modern Parisian life of the 1870s, he presented all aspects of it as if they were equally harmonious and untroubled.   J.H.

Pierre-Auguste Renoir (1841–1919)

Portrait of Ambroise Vollard 1908

Oil on canvas, 81.6 × 65.2
Signed, upper left: 'Renoir. 08'
Samuel Courtauld Collection

Renoir met the young dealer Vollard around 1895; born on the island of Réunion, Vollard began to buy from Renoir, and after 1900 became one of the principal dealers in his work, though in retrospect his main claim to fame is as the organiser of the first extensive exhibitions of Cézanne's work, from 1895 onwards. Vollard was later to write important books on both Renoir and Cézanne.

Vollard commissioned portraits of himself from many of the artists whose work he bought – from Cézanne, Picasso, Bonnard and others. Of all these, Renoir's is one of the least acute, either as a record of the dealer's ugly, bulldog features, or as an evocation of his cunning, quirky personality. Rather, Renoir chose to make his picture into an image of an archetypal connoisseur, appreciatively holding a statuette, very much in the tradition of such collector portraits of the Italian Renaissance.

Vollard is shown holding a statuette by Aristide Maillol, the *Crouching Woman* of 1900, apparently in its original plaster form. It was around this time that Maillol, at Vollard's request, visited Renoir to execute a portrait bust of him, and the inclusion of the piece by Maillol here may refer to this. Moreover, the simplified, monumental classicism which Maillol evolved from the late 1890s onwards may well be relevant to the development of Renoir's art during these years. In the 1890s, he had looked in particular to the Rococo painters of the French eighteenth century, but after 1900 he seems deliberately to have adopted a broader treatment and a more monumental type of composition and modelling – a sort of timeless classicism.

This development appears in *Portrait of Ambroise Vollard* in the firmly modelled, rounded treatment of the figure, far more distinctly separated from its surroundings than the figures in *La Loge*, and also in his return to grey and black as a means of modelling; black had still been used in *La Loge*, but in the mid-1870s he largely abandoned it, using it only when a particular commission demanded it, in favour of modelling suggested by the play of colour alone. He re-adopted black in the 1890s, partly as a result of his studies of the techniques of the old masters, and thereafter he insisted that it was a colour of prime importance in his palette. In this portrait, the comparatively monochrome treatment of the jacket, enriched only by a few coloured nuances on the folds, is set off against the warmth of the flesh modelling and the background. In marked contrast to his earlier work, blue is only very sparingly used, appearing only at a few points on the tablecloth and in the pottery on the table.

J.H.

Eugène Boudin (1824–98)

Deauville 1893

Oil on canvas, 50.8 × 74.2
Signed, lower left: 'Deauville/E. Boudin 93'
Samuel Courtauld Collection

In 1862 Boudin began to paint fashionable figures on the beaches of the celebrated holiday resorts of Trouville and Deauville on the Normandy coast. In his previous paintings he had explored the coastline around his home town of Le Havre, just across the Seine estuary from Trouville, but it was with this genre of modern life beach scene that he won a reputation. In 1868 he wrote to his friend M. Martin: 'These gentlemen congratulate me for having dared to put down on canvas the things and people of our own time, for having found the way to gain acceptance for men in great-coats and women in waterproofs. . . . The peasants have their favoured painters . . . but the bourgeois who walk on the jetty towards the sunset, don't they have the right to be fixed on canvas, to be brought out into the light?'

He worked on the beaches in a variety of media – in pencil and watercolours as well as oils. His more elaborate paintings of such figure subjects were very probably reworked, or indeed entirely executed, in the studio. In his later work, Boudin concentrated more on the open panoramas of the Normandy beaches than on the holidaymakers who peopled them. The figures here are rapidly indicated – holidaymakers, it seems, over by the water, working men with their cart and horses on the left – so that we sense the varied uses of the beach. But light and atmosphere form the principal subject of the painting.

Though Boudin had worked closely with Monet in the 1860s, and exhibited in the first group exhibition in 1874, he never fully adopted the broken touch and lavish atmospheric colour of the Impressionists. His brushwork remained rather tighter and more graphic, suggesting forms and textures very delicately, and his colour more restrained, though nuances of blue and green are used here to suggest the forms in the distance. In this sense, Boudin remained faithful to the *peinture claire*, the luminous, blonde painting, of which he had been a pioneer in the 1850s.

By this refined touch and colour, Boudin managed to evoke the vast scale of the beach and sky, bearing witness to the skills which led Corot to christen him the 'king of skies'. However, the execution of the canvas was a more complex business than appears at first sight. Where the primed canvas is visible in the sky area, it shows a speckled worn surface, indicating that it was rubbed or scraped down in order to reduce an early paint layer, a blue which shares signs of this abrasion, and the process inevitably removed the upmost ridges of the canvas weave. The present state of the sky for all its apparent freshness, is thus a thorough revision of the painting's original effect and exploits the partial retention of the underlying blue layer.   J.H.

Paul Cézanne (1839–1906)

The Montagne Sainte-Victoire c.1887

Oil on canvas, 66.8 × 92.3
Signed, lower right: 'P. Cezanne'
Samuel Courtauld Collection

The Montagne Sainte-Victoire lies to the east of Cézanne's birthplace, Aix-en-Provence, and from many points of view its broken silhouette dominates the town. Cézanne painted it from many viewpoints throughout his career, and it was clearly a subject to which he attributed great significance. In this composition, it is seen from a vantage point to the west of Aix, near Cézanne's family home, the Jas de Bouffan, with the valley of the Arc in the foreground and an aqueduct to the far right; the mountain peak lies about eight miles from this viewpoint, but Cézanne, by focusing on a comparatively small part of the scene in front of him, gave the mountain its dominant role in the composition.

When this painting, along with a *Champ de blé*, was shown by invitation at the exhibition of the Société des Amis des Arts at Aix (a society of amateur artists) in 1895, it was received with incomprehension, but it attracted the admiration of the young poet Joachim Gasquet, son of a childhood friend of Cézanne; when Cézanne realised that the young man's praise was sincere, he signed the picture and presented it to him, initiating a friendship which lasted until around 1904. It is one of the very few paintings from after 1880 to which Cézanne added his signature. In 1908, two years after Cézanne's death, Gasquet sold it for the very high price of 12,000 francs to the dealers Bernheim-Jeune.

In comparison with earlier work, the picture shows a simplification of Cézanne's painting technique. Traces of his system of parallel brushstrokes remain, particularly in some of the foliage, but elsewhere the paint areas are flatter and less variegated, with soft nuances of colour introduced to suggest surface texture and the play of light. In places the cream priming of the canvas is left bare, and its luminosity contributes to the overall tonality of the picture. Traces of the initial and extensive underdrawing, in Prussian blue paint, remain visible in the final state of the painting.

Recession into distance is suggested by the gradual transition from the clearer greens and orange-yellows of the foreground to the softer atmospheric blues and pinks on the mountain, but even the foreground foliage is repeatedly tinged with blues, and pinks and reds – notably on the branch silhouetted against the sky – knit the foreground forms to the far mountain. The placing of the branches, carefully framing the contour of the mountain, enhances this surface coherence. Small touches of red were added in several parts of the composition at a late stage in its execution in order to emphasise these interconnections, most conspicuously, the crisp red stroke on the roof of the tiny building about four inches above the bottom centre of the canvas. The treatment of the whole picture, with zones of cooler and warmer colour virtually alternating as the viewer's eye moves up its surface and into space, transforms its natural subject into a composition of great order and monumentality.

J.H.

Paul Cézanne (1839–1906)

Still Life with Plaster Cast c.1894

Oil on paper, laid on board, 70.6 × 57.3
Samuel Courtauld Collection

Cézanne's still lifes perhaps reveal his changing preoccupations most fully, since still life gave him the freedom to choose and arrange the combinations of objects he wanted to depict. A witness described the complex business of setting up one such still life subject:

> The cloth was arranged on the table, with innate taste. Then Cézanne arranged the fruits, contrasting the tones one against the other, making the complementaries vibrate, the greens against the reds, the yellows against the blues, tipping, turning, balancing the fruit as he wanted them to be, using coins of one or two sous for the purpose. He brought to this task the greatest care and many precautions; one guessed it was a feast for the eye to him.

Still Life with Plaster Cast is one of the most complex of his late still lifes, both in its composition and through the inclusion of the cast and other works of art. The plaster cast of a Cupid (formerly attributed to Pierre Puget) still remains in Cézanne's studio at Aix, as does the cast of a flayed man which is seen in the painting at the top of the present picture. The Cupid cast is in reality eighteen inches high, and it appears larger than life in the painting; the same is true of the canvas which is shown leaning against the wall on the left, *Still Life with Peppermint Bottle* (National Gallery of Art, Washington) which was painted at much the same time as this picture; the area of it that we see, which includes the red stripe and blue area at top left, is shown here larger than it is in the original canvas, although implicitly it is standing on the floor well beyond the foreground table. The far apple, apparently placed on the distant floor, appears as large as the fruit on the table.

There are ambiguities, too, in the relationships between the objects. The 'real' blue drapery at the bottom left merges with the painted still life in the picture on the left; the foliage of the 'real' onion fuses with the table leg in the same still life; and the back edge of the table top virtually dissolves into the floor to the left of this onion. There is also real uncertainty about the arrangement of planes in the background, where the edges of the canvas depicting the flayed figure cannot be clearly determined.

The inconsistencies and paradoxes of the space are compounded by the paradoxes about the nature of the reality depicted which recur throughout the picture: between 'real' and painted fruit and drapery; between 'real' fruit on the table and the Cupid figure – a cast of a statue; and between this cast and the flayed man beyond – a painting of a cast of a statue. All of these devices seem to stress the artificiality of the picture itself – of its grouping and of its making; of all Cézanne's still lifes, this one reveals most vividly the artificiality of the idea of *nature morte*, an assemblage of objects, arranged in order to be painted, and, beyond this, the artifice of the art of painting itself.

J.H.

Paul Cézanne (1839–1906)

The Lac d'Annecy 1896

Oil on canvas, 65 × 81
Samuel Courtauld Collection

The Lac d'Annecy was painted while Cézanne was on holiday at Talloires on the shores of this lake in Haute-Savoie in July 1896; the view is taken from the beach of Talloires, looking in a southerly direction towards the Château de Duingt, half hidden by trees on the far side of the lake. Cézanne wrote in a letter to Gasquet from Talloires: 'This is a temperate zone. The surrounding hills are quite lofty. The lake, which at this point narrows to a bottleneck, seems to lend itself to the line drawing exercises of young ladies. Certainly it is still a bit of nature, but a little like we've been taught to see it in the albums of young lady travellers.' In this canvas, with its vibrant colour and monumental structure, Cézanne was clearly determined to transcend this commonplace picturesque.

The large part of the canvas is dominated by a cool colour range of blues and greens, sometimes quite deep and sonorous in tone, but its principal focuses are the succession of warm accents which run across it, where the early morning sunshine strikes the objects in the scene – the far hills, the left tree trunk, and the buildings across the water. This warm-cool contrast is brought into particularly sharp focus on the left edge of the castle tower: a vertical stroke of orange is set against the deep blues beyond, but, between the two, there is an extremely narrow band of canvas, only very thinly painted with very pale hues so that the building is lifted forward from its surroundings both by the stroke of warm colouring and by this sharp thread of light. The decision not to overpaint this fine streak at the point that he added colour on either side of it shows how tightly he controlled the colour effects he achieved.

The whole picture is carefully structured, with the massive bulk of the tree as a *repoussoir* on the left and its branches enclosing the top; the composition is anchored in the centre by the tighter, more rectilinear forms of the buildings and their elongated reflections. In reality, the castle is about one mile away across the water from Cézanne's viewpoint, but, by narrowing his visual field and focusing closely on it, he made it seem considerably closer (compare the mountain in *The Montagne Sainte-Victoire*). The reflections are slightly distorted – they are not exactly vertical; Cézanne often ignored discrepancies of this sort as he concentrated on the relationships of colour and form in his canvases.

The brushwork across the background builds up a sequence of planes of colour, which unite the nearby foliage to the far hillsides. This means of giving a unified structure to the whole surface became even more prominent in Cézanne's last works, but it was not a means of rejecting nature; rather he sought, he said, a 'harmony parallel to nature' and to 'revivify Poussin in front of nature'; it was thus that he hoped to make out of his experiences of the visible world a lasting, coherent art.   J.H.

Paul Cézanne (1839–1906)

'Route tournante' 1902–6

Oil on canvas, 73 × 92
Princes Gate Collection

Painted during the last four years of the artist's life, this picture was acquired by the dealer Ambroise Vollard either direct from Cézanne, or from his son, soon after the artist's death. It remained in Vollard's possession until Sir Kenneth (later Lord) Clark bought it in about 1937, and it was from Clark that Count Seilern purchased it in August 1941. The stretcher bears a pencil inscription 'Village et Eglise', possibly in Vollard's handwriting, but Lionello Venturi published this painting as 'Route tournante', and this title has been retained.

The location cannot be identified with complete precision, but comparison with other late works such as the *Garden of Les Lauves*, where a similar broad expanse of horizontal bands of terrain appears, suggests that this painting may be a view from Cézanne's studio at Les Lauves which stands on high ground to the north of Aix-en-Provence. He occupied this studio from September 1902 until his death in October 1906, and Marianne Bourges, curator of the Atelier Cézanne at Les Lauves, has suggested that the view in this painting is of the Chemin de Mazenot on the outskirts of Aix, looking west from Les Lauves. On the eastern side, in Cézanne's day, a view of the Montagne Sainte-Victoire could be seen; to the south lay Aix. The church steeple does not appear to resemble that of S. Jean de Malte at all closely, and the church lies on the south side of the town centre. If it were a view looking south, then one would expect more of the town to be visible. All the area around Les Lauves has been intensively developed in recent years and the views once enjoyed by Cézanne are now hidden by high-rise buildings.

The colourman and dealer, Père Tanguy, noted Cézanne's habit in his later years of apparently leaving canvases unfinished, but it can also be argued that in works like 'Route tournante', Cézanne uses the colour of the white-primed canvas as part of the overall matrix of tonal construction. His late watercolours, such as the Courtauld *Still Life with Apples, Bottle and Chairback*, show a similar preoccupation, where the white paper is allowed to appear as integral to the composition. In other words, Cézanne took the painting to a stage of completeness which satisfied his ideal of a tautly constructed web of colour and forms, where the predominantly vertical brushstrokes act as a visual counterpoint to the horizontal format of the composition.

There is no discernible varnish on the painting and much of the ground, originally white, is exposed and has in places a mottled appearance common in Cézanne's late work. This effect is probably caused by the discoloration of some constituent in the ground.   D.F.

94

Georges Seurat (1859–91)

The Bridge at Courbevoie 1886–7

Oil on canvas, 46.4 × 55.3
Signed, lower left: 'Seurat'
Samuel Courtauld Collection

The Bridge at Courbevoie is one of the clearest pictorial manifestoes for the divisionist painting technique evolved by Seurat and his colleagues in 1885–6. The technique was intended as a means of translating into paint the effects of natural light and colour, lending a scientific precision to the more empirical solutions that had been adopted by Monet and Pissarro. The dot, or point, of colour was the means which seemed best able to control precisely the relative quantities of each colour used in any area of the picture. Camille Pissarro, at the time that he was closely associated with Seurat, stated that the optimum viewing distance for a picture was three times its diagonal measurement, which in this case would mean seven feet. The effect of the canvas from this distance is that the dots are still clearly visible as dots, and the varied colours included can still be identified separately; far from fusing, they seem to shimmer and vibrate – in a sense to recreate in the eye of the viewer something of the sense of vibration produced by actual outdoor sunlight.

In *The Bridge at Courbevoie*, Seurat's analysis of the different elements present in a light effect is most evident in the treatment of the river bank. The dominant colour is green – the 'local' colour of grass – rather lighter and yellower in the sunlight, duller and bluer in shadow; warm, pinker touches further enliven the sunlit grass, and clear blues the shadowed areas. In addition there is a scatter of mauve touches across most of the shadowed grass, and they reappear in the topmost band of sunlit grass, along the edge of the river. Their effect is to enhance the play of warm and cool colours, whose elaborately interwoven relationships give the surface its richness and mobility. The background is treated with softer, paler hues, the same colour repeating in many parts of the picture.

The scene represents the Ile de la Grande Jatte, looking south westwards, upstream along the Seine towards the Courbevoie bridge. In contrast to the elaborate parade of modern society in the *Sunday Afternoon on the Ile de la Grande Jatte*, *The Bridge at Courbevoie* is still and silent, with three small figures standing immobile by the river. Its mood seems elusive and difficult to interpret; though it has recently been described as a 'plangent evocation of melancholy and alienation'. The picture retains an intriguing strangeness through its very stillness, and through the curious juxtaposition of the foliated trees on the left, and the stark bare branches on the right. All the elements in it are presented in an ordered, harmonious coexistence; the vertical of the central factory chimney is closely paralleled by the boats' masts and the fence-posts, establishing with the figures a taut series of pictorial intervals.

There is a further oddity about the picture: the verticals of the chimney, the masts and the house on the far right are all inclined at a slight but perceptible angle to the left. Seurat organised his compositions with such care that this cannot have been accidental, and its effect, it seems, is to emphasise the parallel lines within the picture, for the viewer's eye does not immediately relate them to the grid of the picture frame around them. It may have been begun out of doors, but its final effect can only have been achieved in the studio.   J.H.

Georges Seurat (1859–91)

Young Woman Powdering Herself c.1888–90

Oil on canvas, 95.5 × 79.5
Signed, on painted border, lower right: 'Seurat'
Samuel Courtauld Collection

This is the only one of Seurat's paintings which reflects anything about his private existence; it shows his mistress, Madeleine Knobloch, at her toilette. Apparently Seurat's own face originally appeared in the frame on the wall, but a friend warned him that this might appear laughable and he replaced it with the vase of flowers. Examination of the painting under the microscope and of the X-ray clearly show that the artist did obliterate a previous reflection in the mirror, but an interpretation of these vague outlines as the face of Seurat himself is highly subjective.

The painting is composed of a sequence of contrasts between rounded and angular forms: the figure and table are set against the wall with its picture frame and arrow-shaped patterns; and it plays on a set of visual incongruities – between the massive figure and her impracticably small table (the *poudreuse* by which the picture has sometimes been incorrectly named), and between the curving lines and pseudo-dix-huitième ornament of this table and the imitation bamboo frame above it.

Seurat left no indication of the picture's meaning, but it contains many instances of his sign for happiness and gaiety: the motif of lines rising from a point, which is used here to decorate the wall. The motif on the wall is echoed by the bow on top of the mirror, the frame top, the plant form at lower left, and even the model's right arm and the curl of hair behind her neck. But Seurat does not use these directional lines to uplift the spirits of the viewer so much as to suggest irony. They all belong to her personal décor, to her furniture and cosmetics; the weighty model and her impassive expression counteract them.

The painting explores the contrast between nature and artifice: the art of cosmetics, which, like the model's corsetry, force nature into the mould of style; the spectator, viewing her in mid-toilette, catches her in the middle of the process making her natural self artificial. The satire is not, though, directed against the model herself, but rather against her trappings, which were so characteristic a part of modern urban life.

In contrast to *The Bridge at Courbevoie*, the brushwork and colours here do not evoke the play of natural light and shade. Rather, they are used to augment the pictorial impact of the canvas. The background wall becomes darker and bluer where it approaches lit contours of the figure, and lighter where it meets its shadowed edges; throughout the picture there is an eddy of interwoven warm and cool touches (pinks and yellows against blues and greens) which create a shimmering effect over the whole surface, but without in any way suggesting closely observed lighting. The painted border augments this effect. The modelling of the figure is wilfully anti-naturalistic; it is impossible to sense the form of the model's hips and legs within the sweeping, stylised curves of her skirt. The dots of colour, though comparatively even in size, are often slightly elongated and follow the contours of the forms; it is evident that this final skin of colour was applied over more broadly applied, initial layers of paint, as Seurat worked up the picture to completion. J.H.

Vincent van Gogh (1853–90)

Portrait of the Artist with bandaged Ear 1889

Oil on canvas, 60.5 × 50
Samuel Courtauld Collection

This is probably the earlier of the two *Self-Portraits* van Gogh painted in Arles in January 1889. He appears here noticeably more pale and haggard than in the version which belonged to Mr. and Mrs. Leigh Block of Chicago.

The portrait epitomises the tragic instability that marked much of the artist's working life and which led to his suicide, by shooting, on 29 July 1890. He had gone to Arles in the early Spring of 1888 where he was later joined by Paul Gauguin. For a while the two painters lived together amicably, but van Gogh, in December 1888, began to suffer from hallucinations and on 24 December, after a violent quarrel with Gauguin, whilst 'in a state of terrible excitement', cut off a piece of his own ear. He was admitted to hospital at Arles on the same day and stayed there under supervision and receiving treatment until about 6 January 1889, when he returned to his own house. Writing to his brother, Theo, on 9 January he recorded that he had been 'again at the hospital to get another dressing', and he seems to have begun work again that same day. By 17 January he told his brother he had completed four pictures, reworked another, and had completed 'another new' *Self Portrait*. Only two *Self-Portraits* of this period are known, one of which is the Courtauld painting.

The later history of the picture can be traced from the dealer and colourman, Père Tanguy of Paris, a friend of many of the Impressionist artists, and it was presumably bought by him from van Gogh. It then passed to Count A. de la Rochefoucauld, Paris, and was with the dealer, Paul Rosenberg, before Samuel Courtauld acquired it in 1928. He bequeathed it to the Courtauld Institute of Art in January 1948.

The portrait is of particular interest for the evidence it provides of links between Japanese and Western European art. Van Gogh had been influenced by Toulouse-Lautrec and, probably through him, had his interest aroused in Japanese Ukioyē coloured woodcuts, an interest shared by many of the Impressionist and Post-Impressionist artists in France, and by James McNeill Whistler and artists of the Aesthetic Movement in England. The strongly marked, rhythmic outlines in this portrait, and its flattened perspective, undoubtedly owe something to the conventions of Japanese popular art, but even more telling is the presence on the wall behind the artist, of a print attributed to Sato Torakiyo, *Geishas in a Landscape*. A copy of this print belonged to van Gogh.

Van Gogh's painting techniques were sometimes imperfect, and this portrait is no exception. It is in an extremely fragile state and a previous relining treatment has now made it impossible to stabilize the adhesion of the paint layers to the canvas support by wax impregnation. D.F.

Vincent van Gogh (1853–90)

Peach Blossom in the Crau 1889

Oil on canvas, 65 × 81
Samuel Courtauld Collection

Painted in Arles in March–April 1889, this canvas shows a view of the Crau, the wide plain which lies to the north-east of Arles, between the river Rhône and the Alpilles – the range of hills that encloses the background of the picture. Van Gogh enclosed a rough pen sketch of the composition in a letter to Paul Signac, and described the picture:

> I have just come back with two studies of orchards. Here is a crude sketch of them – the big one is a poor landscape with little cottages, blue skyline of the Alpille foothills, sky white and blue. The foreground, patches of land surrounded by cane hedges, where small peach trees are in bloom – everything is small there, the gardens, the fields, the orchards and the trees, even the mountains, as in certain Japanese landscapes, which is the reason why the subject attracted me.

The idea of the south of France as a western equivalent of Japan had been one of van Gogh's main reasons for travelling to Arles the previous year; here, the seemingly snowcapped peak in the right background may be an echo of Mount Fuji-Yama.

Peach Blossom in the Crau was painted after Gauguin's visit to Arles, during which he had advised van Gogh to work from his imagination and not directly from the natural subject. But after Gauguin's departure, van Gogh reasserted his commitment to painting from nature, here returning to the approximate subject of one of his major works of the previous summer, *The Blue Cart* (Rijksmuseum Vincent van Gogh, Amsterdam); in contrast to Gauguin's schematic paint surfaces, van Gogh conveys the complex textures and patterns of the chosen scene with a great variety of brushmarks, some broad and incisive, but others of extreme finesse. The laden dabs of paint in the blossom reflect his study of Impressionist painting during his stay in Paris but elsewhere the forms are far crisper and more clearly drawn, particularly in the web of very fine, dark red strokes added in many parts of the picture very late in its execution in order to emphasise the forms of the elements shown – in the houses, the trees and the foreground verge. Added very late, too, was the sequence of blue strokes on the road at the bottom, together with blue accents elsewhere in the landscape and sky, which serve to knit the main elements of the scene together into an atmospheric unity, whose keynote is the vivid blues of the far mountains and the lower band of the sky.

In its translation of this display of blossom into a rich coloured harmony, the picture is clearly indebted to Impressionism; yet its subject also reflects van Gogh's Dutch heritage. He often likened the wide spaces of the Crau with the panoramas of Dutch 17th-century landscape painting. In the inclusion of the working figure on the left of *Peach Blossom in the Crau*, along with the prominent small houses, van Gogh emphasised that this was a social, agricultural landscape, its forms the result of man's intervention. Of the Impressionists, Pissarro was always concerned to emphasise the human context of his chosen landscape subjects, whereas Monet was by the later 1880s concentrating primarily on effects of light and atmosphere.

J.H.

Paul Gauguin (1848–1903)

Nevermore 1897

Oil on canvas, 60.5 × 116
Signed, top left: 'NEVERMORE/P.Gauguin 97/0. TAÏTÍ'
Samuel Courtauld Collection

Gauguin painted *Nevermore* in February 1897, during his second visit to Tahiti. He described the painting in a letter to Daniel de Monfreid, the fellow-painter who was acting as his agent in Paris:

> I wished to suggest by means of a simple nude a certain long-lost barbarian luxury. The whole is drowned in colours which are deliberately sombre and sad; it is neither silk, nor velvet, nor *batiste*, nor gold that creates luxury here but simply matter that has been enriched by the hand of the artist. No nonsense . . . Man's imagination alone has enriched the dwelling with his fantasy. As a title, Nevermore; not the raven of Edgar Poe, but the bird of the devil that is keeping watch. It is badly painted (I'm so nervy and can only work in bouts) but no matter, I think it's a good canvas.

Nevermore belongs to a long tradition of reclining female nudes. The pose, with the exaggerated curve of the figure's hip, perhaps echoes the sensuous exoticism of Ingres' *Odalisque with a Slave*, but whereas the luxury in Ingres' picture is presented as tranquil and undisturbed, Gauguin produces an image as complex and challenging as that other pioneering avant-garde odalisque, Manet's *Olympia* (of which Gauguin had a photograph in his hut in Tahiti). But, whereas Manet's picture confronts the subject of public sexuality and prostitution in the modern city, *Nevermore* explores in a more allusive way more private realms of sensual experience.

The painting sets up a triangular relationship between the nude figure, the bird, seemingly watching, and the clothed figures in the background, turned away and talking. The turn of the nude's eyes suggests that she is aware of the bird or the other figures, but beyond this nothing is clear. The contrast of unclothed with clothed, of reverie with conversation, may evoke the loss of innocence. The image should be understood not just as the awakening of a particular woman, but rather in the context of the corruption of 'primitive' cultures – Oceanic Gardens of Eden – by the influx of western values. A corruption Gauguin had himself witnessed on Tahiti.

The bird's role, too, is ambiguous. Though in his letter Gauguin played down its relationship to Poe's *Raven*, the bird, in conjunction with the title, would inevitably have evoked Poe's poem for the painting's original viewers; Poe's work was widely known in artistic circles in Paris in the late 19th century, and Mallarmé's translation of the *Raven*, illustrated by Manet, had appeared in 1875. Gauguin may well have sought to minimise this association in order to avoid too explicitly literary a reference, but the bird's presence here is as ominous as in the poem, in which it stands above the poet's door, croaking 'Nevermore'; in the picture, it contributes, with the conversing figures, to the sense of threat which invades the luxury of the nude's surroundings.

The allusive elements in the interior, as Gauguin's letter insists, are imagined. They were integral to Gauguin's idea of Symbolism; he wrote in 1899, quoting Mallarmé, of one of his paintings as a 'musical poem without a libretto', insisting that it could not be read allegorically. The sharp yellow of the nude's pillow and the red by her feet heighten her strangeness and further separate her from her surroundings, but cannot be interpreted literally. The iconic quality of the whole picture is enhanced by its smooth, dense surface (in marked contrast to *Te Rerioa*), but Gauguin exploits this effect which was caused by his painting over another quite different subject; he found that the presence of these dense underlying layers allowed him to give the picture a distinctive physical quality.

The English composer Frederick Delius was the first owner of the painting. Gauguin wrote to de Monfreid in 1899 to express his pleasure that Delius had bought it 'given that it is not a speculative purchase for re-sale, but for enjoyment'. J.H.

Paul Gauguin (1848–1903)

Te Rerioa 1897

Oil on canvas, 95.1 × 130.2
Signed, lower left centre:
'TE RERIOA/P. Gauguin 97/TAÏTÍ'
Samuel Courtauld Collection

Te Rerioa was painted in Tahiti in March 1897, about three weeks after *Nevermore*. Some of the forms shown on the walls of the room bear some relationship to Gauguin's surviving wood carvings, but it is probable that the decorations were largely imaginary, created as appropriate décor for the picture, as in *Nevermore*.

Gauguin described the painting in a letter when he despatched it to Daniel de Monfreid in France: 'Te Rereioa (the Dream), that is the title. Everything is dream in this canvas; is it the child? is it the mother? is it the horseman on the path? or even is it the dream of the painter!!! All that is incidental to painting, some will say. Who knows. Maybe it isn't.' The spelling of the Tahitian title in this letter is correct; it is wrongly spelt on the canvas. The word in fact means nightmare, but, as he wrote, Gauguin was using it more generally to mean dream.

The uncertainties which Gauguin here playfully spelt out are integral to the painting, since no figures communicate with each other, and none has a clearly legible expression. The image is made up from a set of contrasts: sleeping child and daydreaming women; sleeping child and the seemingly active, carved figure on the cradle; the women seated still and the figures making love in the wall decoration; these figures seated passively and the active man, riding on the path and placed precisely between the heads of the two women; live animal on the floor beside carved animal on the wall decoration.

But Gauguin's letter reminds us that none of these elements is 'real', for all are the creation of the painter who has conjured up this series of puzzles and possibilities; this is emphasised by the physical appearance of the painting itself – thinly and broadly painted over coarse sacking, so that its flatness and the physical presence of the paint and the sacking are constantly apparent.

In its ambiguities, and also in the qualities of its surface, this canvas, perhaps more than any other by Gauguin, answers the requirements of the poet Stéphane Mallarmé for a true 'symbol'. In an interview in 1891, Mallarmé stated:

> I think that there should only be allusion. The contemplation of objects, the image emanating from the dreams they excite, this is poetry. . . . To *suggest*, that is the dream. That is the perfect use of mystery that constitutes symbol.

A painting such as *Te Rerioa* was intended for a European audience, presenting an archetype of 'primitive' reverie in unspoilt surroundings, and a fusion of eroticism and innocence. This vision bore no relation to the state of society in Tahiti in the 1890s but the picture was a contribution to a long European tradition of images of the 'noble savage'; particularly relevant to *Te Rerioa* was perhaps Delacroix's *Women of Algiers* (1834; Musée du Louvre, Paris), in which sensuous reverie was sited in a North African Orientalist context. These visions owe their origins not to the 'primitive' worlds they show, but to the reactions of European artists against the complexities of modern urban society; the idylls they create from the 'otherness' of their material belong firmly in the west, as projections of dissatisfaction with the values of western society.　　J.H.

Henri de Toulouse-Lautrec (1864–1901)

Jane Avril in the Entrance of the Moulin Rouge, drawing on her Gloves 1892

Pastel and oil on millboard, laid on panel, 102 × 55.1
Signed, lower left, initials in monogram: 'HT-Lautrec'
Samuel Courtauld Collection

Jane Avril was a celebrated popular dancer, reportedly the illegitimate daughter of an Italian nobleman and a Parisian demi-mondaine, who first appeared at the Moulin Rouge in 1889, and became one of its star performers. She was nicknamed *La Mélinite* – the name of a recently invented form of explosive. She was one of Lautrec's favourite models, and became his close friend and supporter. Often he depicted her dancing; the English poet Arthur Symons described his first experience of watching her dance in 1892: 'Young and girlish, the more provocative because she played as a prude, with an assumed modesty, *décolletée* nearly to the waist, in the Oriental fashion. She had about her an air of depraved virginity.' But here Lautrec showed her in street clothes, either arriving at or leaving a performance. The thinness of the figure is emphasised by the elongated format – created by the addition of a large extra piece of millboard at the bottom. The apparent immateriality of her figure is wittily set against the looming presence of the male hat and coat seen on the left, apparently hanging on the wall alongside Jane Avril.

The experimental combination of techniques here is comparable to methods pioneered by Degas. Lautrec laid in broad areas of the picture in oil, while the pastel elaboration allowed him to combine colour and drawing – simultaneously to sharpen the indication of the forms and to enrich the play of colour; this is most conspicuous around the figure's face and hat, where finer strokes of reds, yellows and greens are set off against the bold slashes of blue paint in the right background. These sharp colour relationships, and the pallid yellow which lights the figure's face, heighten the sense of the artificiality of this world of urban entertainments.   J.H.

Amedeo Modigliani (1884–1920)

Female Nude c.1916

Oil on canvas, 92.4 × 59.8
Signed, upper left: 'Modigliani'
Samuel Courtauld Collection

Modigliani's nudes are a combination of poses which often relate to the main traditions of western art (to Manet, Ingres and other earlier artists) with a type of drawing and execution which in its radical simplifications challenged the whole European figurative tradition. In *Female Nude*, the face is elongated, its features boldly simplified, in ways which testify to Modigliani's knowledge of Egyptian, African and Oceanic sculpture, though in a generalised way; yet the angle of the model's head recalls the very conventional imagery of the sleeping model, a favourite theme at the Salon exhibitions. Likewise the contours and modelling of the body are treated in simplified arabesques, but elements such as the breasts and especially the pubic hair are described more attentively. Modigliani's brushwork is highly individual; characteristic scallop-shaped strokes can be seen in the X-radiograph, the paint being applied with a short stabbing action. The paint has been manipulated while still wet, ploughed through with a stiff brush in the background left and around the outline of the head, and scratched into with the end of the brush in the hair.

When a group of Modigliani's nudes were put on show at Berthe Weill's gallery in Paris in December 1917, the police first ordered the removal of the painting in the gallery window, and then the closure of the whole exhibition; apparently the prime cause of outrage was his explicit rendering of pubic hair, a taboo in the often very naturalistic depictions of the nude which hung every year at the Salon without any protests. It is noteworthy that this painting, with its combination of traditional and avant-garde elements, was the only painting in Samuel Courtauld's collection by a member of one of the avant-garde groups which emerged after 1900; Cubism and even Fauvism were outside the parameters of his taste.   J.H.

Oskar Kokoschka (1886–1980)

Market in Tunis 1928–9

Oil on canvas, 86.5 × 129
Princes Gate Collection

On 5 January 1928 Kokoschka arrived in Tunis from Marseilles. There, from the roof of a greengrocer's shop on Place Bab Souika, he painted this townscape. To a friend, three days after his arrival, he wrote: 'From 1–6 I paint, by the evening I'm tired, so go to bed at 9, then in the mornings from 9–12 I have 'flu, so stay in bed.' In his autobiography, *My Life*, he himself describes what is shown in the painting, the 'magnificent view of the great mosque and the adjoining square, with its procession of weddings, funerals and circumcisions. Swaying camels and heavy-laden donkeys swung through the dark alleys of the souk beneath me; clouds of flies swarmed around the butchers' shops and sweetmeat stalls. A week later, with the painting almost completed, I fell through the roof of the shop, easel and all; even after lengthy bargaining, I had to pay the proprietor a considerable sum of money for a new roof.' At this point the canvas was rolled up and carried about by the travelling artist, as witness the three sets of nail holes along the edges, the damage and paint losses as well as the 'foreign' paint stuck to it. The painting was completed the following year in Asia Minor.

From 1923 to 1930 Kokoschka travelled widely, painting 'travel pictures' – landscapes and townscapes – in eleven different European countries as well as in North Africa and Asia Minor. He was financed by his Berlin agents, Cassirer. Whenever possible Kokoschka sought a high point, a hill or tall building, to obtain the broad views he preferred; he also on occasion used two different viewpoints to increase the impression evident in many of his townscapes, including this one, of a sweeping curved movement, a wide-angled vision. Fine portraits of this period include those of Arabs, as well as that of the Hungarian collector, Marczell von Nemeš, the first owner of the *Market in Tunis*.

An artist of restless energy and creativity, Kokoschka was born in Austria over a hundred years ago and died in 1980, a British subject, in his adopted Switzerland. Scarred by his experiences in the First World War and a refugee from Nazi condemnation, he was sickened by the inhumanities of this century. Rejecting abstract art, he saw himself as heir to the centuries-old traditions of European art and culture. H.B.

Ben Nicholson (1894–1982)

Painting 1937

Oil on canvas, 79.5 × 91.5
Alastair Hunter Collection

Ben Nicholson painted his first abstract pictures as early as 1924, but it was not until the mid-1930s that he refined his style of all obvious figurative elements. He developed his abstract work in two closely related but distinct media: the white painted low reliefs and easel pictures like *Painting 1937*. Nicholson, and the sculptors Henry Moore and Barbara Hepworth (Nicholson's second wife), were part of a small but influential artistic community living off Haverstock Hill in Hampstead, which included such notable refugee artists as Naum Gabo, who came in 1935, and Piet Mondrian, who arrived in 1938. Nicholson had first visited Mondrian's studio in Paris in 1934, and had been greatly impressed not only by his work, but also by that of Picasso, Braque, Arp, and Brancusi, all of whom he had met on several visits to Paris in the early 1930s.

Nicholson created his first white relief in 1934, and by 1935 his paintings had also become uncompromisingly geometrical. Of his reliefs he wrote: '– a square and a circle are nothing in themselves and are alive only in the instinctive and inspirational use an artist can make of them in expressing a poetic idea . . . You can create a most exciting tension between these forces . . .' (that is to say, the interplay of geometrical forms). This 'most exciting tension' also enlivens his abstract paintings, indeed, one can say all his best work, but it is particularly relevant to *Painting 1937* in which he carefully balances a strong red square and a black rectangle, offsetting them by a brilliant blue linking zone and the surrounding rectangles of softer colours. The overall effect is quite warm and quite different from a larger, related work, also called *Painting 1937* in the Tate Gallery, London, where, despite the use of a black, blue, yellow and red sequence of rectangles on the right hand side of the picture, a sense of coolness prevails.

The genesis of the Courtauld picture and of similar works may be seen in a series of highly geometricised still life on table top compositions, and in yet another *Painting 1937* (Scottish National Gallery of Modern Art, Edinburgh), where vestiges of the table legs are still shown. In some still lifes of 1934, the objects on the table, such as jugs, cups, and plates, appear as highly stylised silhouette-like shapes, with some suggestion of textural variation on the painted surface.

Lady (Leslie) Martin, who once owned this painting, has recalled that the central square of yellow ochre/orange used to be a bright acid-yellow, presumably similar in colour to the yellow rectangle in the Tate painting. The artist must have used some additive to his pigment to cause this unintended change to occur over a period of 50 years.   D.F.

Ivon Hitchens (1893–1979)

Balcony View, Iping Church 1943

Oil on canvas, 105.3 × 51.5
Signed, lower right: 'Hitchens'
Alastair Hunter Collection

This decorative painting, with its unusual vertical format figured alongside twenty-three recent works shown at the Leicester Galleries in 1944. The exhibition was praised by both Clive Bell and by John Piper, who remarked upon Hitchens' 'strong poetic feeling for such things as a damp autumnal landscape'. Hitchens' encounter with Bell's *Since Cézanne*, published in 1922, introduced him to modern French art and subsequently the Bloomsbury ethos and the milieu of the Seven and Five Society. After 1924 Hitchens spent much time with Ben Nicholson, who exhibited a completely abstract work at the Society in 1924 and encouraged a greater experimentation in Hitchens' own work. In October 1929, Hitchens' third one-man show was held at the London Artists' Association, an organisation whose financial supporters included Samuel Courtauld and Maynard Keynes. Hitchens eschewed the development towards geometric abstraction, promoted by the English wing of the Abstraction-Création group (including Piper) and favoured the informal tendencies of the artists whom he joined for the famous 'Objective Abstractions' exhibition at the Zwemmer Gallery in March 1934. The decorative aspects of works such as *Spring Mood*, 1933, which retained references to landscape and flower-pieces, were reinforced in July that year by the one-man show of recent works by Braque at Reid and Lefevre. Although Braque rarely painted flowers and would never have chosen the wild poppies, daisy and clump of coltsfoot in the foreground of *Balcony View, Iping Church*, the pedestal table and wrought-iron balcony device (implying narrow French windows) is highly characteristic of the 1930s French School.

The bright, almost luminous still life, with the poppies aureoled in white, against a chrome yellow background on the right, contrasts strangely with the sombre, melancholy mood of the church in the background and the mixture of autumnal ochres, sienna and purples. The spring flowers evoke a certain Resurrection symbolism in this context (c.f. *Easter Morning*, 1935) and must be read as a symbol of hope in the darkest year of the war. By this time John Piper, having abandoned abstraction, had become the doyen of the English Neo-Romantic movement, which, painting throughout the war, had linked the topographical English landscape tradition – country churches in particular – with a deeply elegaic mode. Iping Church is in West Sussex, near Petworth, where Hitchens had moved when his London house was bombed in 1940. While evidently partaking of this Neo-Romantic spirit, Hitchens' work has a formal daring which distances it from his contemporaries: the bold patches of paint in the upper half of the canvas are very thinly painted with an almost deliberate negligence about edges, creating a white grid which allows light to shine through from 'background' areas. Likewise the overpainted white line vertically slicing the canvas in two suggests a window pane, but vanishes behind the glass of flowers, disrupting a figurative reading as do the vermilion barn roofs on the left which bring distance abruptly forward on to the picture plane.

Avoiding conventional ideas of chiaroscuro, Hitchens, in a note on the 'painter's orchestra' referred to 'formes' (non-representational marks), and 'notan' a Japanese concept of a harmony of darks and lights. Like his better-known works using a horizontal format, *Balcony View, Iping Church* makes an almost perfect double square, insisting upon a scroll-like reading process, in this case both vertical and complicated horizontally by the caesura-like effect of the white line.   s.w.

Andrea Mantegna (1431–1506)

Studies for Christ at the Column early 1460s

Pen and iron gall ink; on grey-buff (discoloured) laid paper.
The sheet trimmed on all sides, and torn, upper left, 23.4 × 14.4
Collector's mark of a lion, stamped in gold, lower right
(unidentified (?)John Skippe: Lugt, 2798; and *Suppl.*, 2798).

Two studies for Christ at the Column, in pen and iron gall ink (*verso*).

Princes Gate Collection

Only 20 examples of Mantegna's drawings have survived. The majority of these, through their close association with finished paintings, can be approximately dated. It seems probable from the nature of this sketch that it was a working study for a painting, although nothing is known of it. A print after this drawing exists which may have been done, either by Mantegna or, as is more likely, by an engraver in his employment.

The majority of Mantegna's drawings are finely executed and highly accomplished studies and are, in all probability, *modelli* for later paintings or for engravings. They differ from the rough, sketchy nature of this work which was swiftly drawn with bold hatching. Only one other example of this style of draughtsmanship is represented in the surviving corpus of Mantegna's drawings and that is the study of S. James being led to Execution now in the British Museum. On this evidence, Mantegna appears to have abandoned the style, c.1464, in favour of the more accomplished and finished quality of his other surviving drawings. It is the immediacy in style of Mantegna's early drawings which has often caused them to be confused with his contemporary and brother-in-law, Giovanni Bellini, a fate which also befell this work at an early stage.

The date of this double-sided drawing is not known but it is believed to have been executed in the early 1460s, probably before 1464. There is no reason to doubt that the two sides of the drawing were not executed at the same time although those figures on the *recto* are technically more finished. It was clearly not produced for sale to a collector and the same subject appears on both sides. The Biblical source for the scene depicted on both sides of this sheet is mentioned briefly by all of the Evangelists. Pontius Pilate ordered that Christ be scourged before being crucified. Nothing is mentioned in the Bible of either a column or beating but the flagellation was an established subject in religious iconography from the early medieval period. Artists usually depicted Christ bound to a column and generally wearing a loincloth. There are usually two or three soldiers with birches, thongs or whips beating Christ on the back. Whereas on the *recto* of Mantegna's drawing the two studies of the standing and dejected Christ show him without any soldiers but bound to a Corinthian column, the flagellation is shown on the *verso*. Here, Mantegna is concerned with the full suffering of Christ and shows him simultaneously from the front and actually being scourged. We see Christ with back bent, suffering under the blows of the nearby soldier. Except for his native Italy, Mantegna's fame as an artist was unjustly neglected in the centuries after his death and his works were sometimes criticised for their dry linearity. Since the 19th century, however, there has been a revival of interest in his works which has lead to his restoration as one of the greatest artists of the quattrocento. c.h.

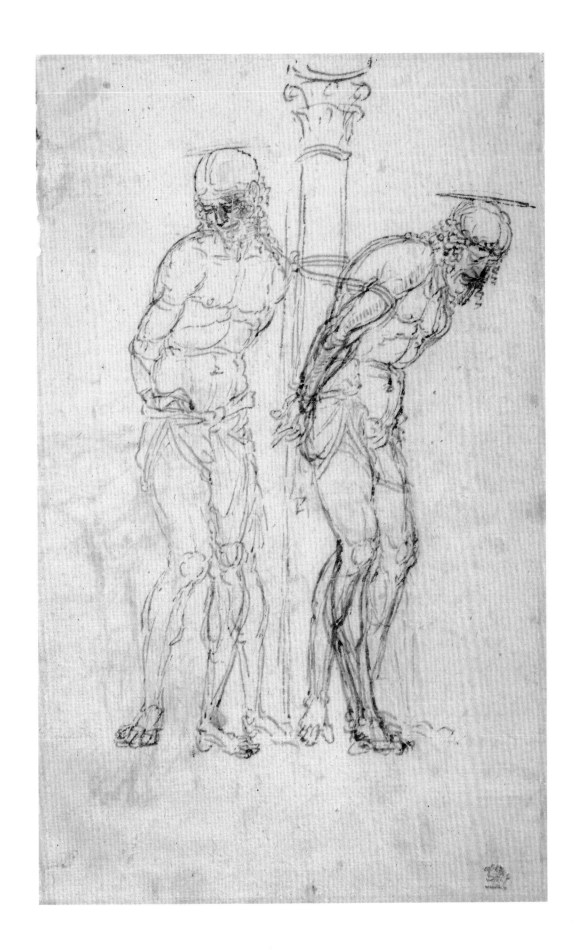

Giovanni Bellini (c.1430–1516)

The Nativity

Pen and iron gall ink; slight drawing with point of brush and iron-gall ink wash; on thin buff laid paper (watermarked with standing bird).
The sheet unevenly trimmed on all sides, the upper corners cut at an angle. Bottom right corner torn away. *Maxima*: 20.1 × 21.2
Inscribed by a later hand in iron gall ink, lower right 'L·', and stamped upper and lower right with collector's mark 'P.L' (Sir Peter Lely: Lugt, 2092).

Princes Gate Collection

There are very few surviving drawings by Giovanni Bellini and their scarcity has made it difficult to establish a corpus of works firmly attributed to him. The problem has been complicated by similarities between drawings by his brother-in-law, Andrea Mantegna, and those thought to be by Bellini, which has resulted in conflicting opinions among scholars of Venetian art.

Johannes Wilde examined both the Mantegna *Studies for Christ at the Column* and Bellini's *Nativity*, and discerned an important stylistic difference between them. The artist has here used pen and ink directly on the sheet, without any preliminary under-drawing, furthermore his 'use of constantly broken, vibrating lines is Bellini's own invention; the colour and light effect produced by this method are startling.' Wilde also considered the composition to be a variant of the painting of *The Nativity*, from the predella of the Pesaro Altarpiece now in the Pesaro Museum, and accepted this drawing as one of Bellini's few composition studies to have come down to us.

The drawing once belonged to the portrait painter Sir Peter Lely, a renowned collector of old master paintings and drawings of the highest quality. After his death in 1680, his drawings were sold in London in two main groups: the first in April 1688 over a period of eight days, which realised about £2400; the second, smaller collection, in November 1694.

D.F.

Hugo van der Goes (active 1467 died 1482)

S. Ursula, seated, holding a Book on her Knees

Pen and ink or watercolour wash for all drawing of principal contours and areas of shadow, with some drawing with the point of the brush in areas of deepest shadow; heightening with pen and the point of the brush in white bodycolour of varying solutions; on off-white laid paper, prepared with a ground of green bodycolour. The sheet laid down, and trimmed on all sides, apparently to lines in graphite, 23 × 18.9
Numbered by a later hand in pen and carbon black ink, lower right: '787' (now partly trimmed away).
Inscriptions by various hands in iron gall ink, *verso*.

Princes Gate Collection

S. Ursula wears a *robe royale*, an outmoded garment retained by ladies of the highest rank for ceremonial occasions. According to legend, S. Ursula was a British princess who, returning from a pilgrimage to Rome, was martyred at Cologne.

A drawing of astonishing assurance, this may be related to a lost painting by van der Goes of the *Virgin and Child with Saints* known from several copies executed in the late 15th and early 16th centuries. Some of the copyists did not follow the original quite accurately and changed the identities of some of the Saints but, if all the versions are compared, it is possible to reconstruct the appearance of the missing picture and to show that the Saint corresponding to the figure in the drawing was Ursula. The figure was also copied in isolation by a great number of painters and illuminators and seems to have influenced Memlinc, who included a rather similar S. Catherine in his *Altarpiece of the Two Saints John*, dated 1479 (Memlinc Museum, Bruges).

The drawing has been thought to be a copy made by van der Goes himself from his lost painting as a record to be kept for future reference in the workshop. It is perhaps more likely to be a preliminary drawing. Infra-red photographs of his *Death of the Virgin* (Bruges) and his *Adoration of the Shepherds* (Berlin) reveal beneath the paint carefully hatched under-drawings which must have been made from elaborate preparatory drawings, themselves based on studies from life. Van der Goes was a perfectionist. In his last years, which he spent at a monastery outside Brussels, 'he was deeply disturbed by the thought of how he could ever finish the works of art which he wanted to paint and it was said that nine years would hardly have been sufficient for him to do so'.

Other drawings, similar in technique but rather less accomplished, have been attributed to van der Goes. The *S. Ursula* is exceptional among 15th-century Netherlandish drawings for its spontaneous sureness of touch. Either the drawing itself, or more probably the lost painting for which it was made, was among the most influential images of the time.   L.C.

Albrecht Dürer (1471–1528)

One of the Wise Virgins 1493

Pen and iron gall ink; on buff laid paper. The sheet unevenly trimmed on all sides, 29 × 20.05
Inscribed by a later hand in iron gall ink, upper centre: '1508 AD' (the date incorrect), and by a modern hand in graphite, lower left: 'G'
Two studies of a man's leg, in pen and iron gall ink, dated by the artist in the same ink, upper centre: '1493' (verso).
Princes Gate Collection

The parable of the Wise and Foolish Virgins was told by Christ to the disciples shortly before the Last Supper (Matthew xxv 1–13). Ten virgins took their lamps to meet a bridegroom. Five were foolish, neglected to provide enough oil for their lamps, had to go to buy more and in so doing missed the bridegroom and the marriage feast, to which the wise virgins, who had brought enough oil, were admitted. A parallel is made between the marriage feast and the Kingdom of Heaven. 'Watch therefore, for ye know neither the day nor the hour wherein the Son of man cometh.' Dürer has shown one of the Wise Virgins carrying her lighted lamp and wearing in her hair a garland for the marriage feast.

The monogram and the date 1508 are not original but on the verso is the genuine date 1493. Dürer was then a journeyman working in Basle and Strasbourg. In 1492 he had visited Colmar, where he had hoped to find the great engraver Martin Schongauer, who had, however, died in 1491. Among Schongauer's prints were ten engravings of full-length figures of the Wise and Foolish Virgins and another of a Foolish Virgin in half-length. Dürer had clearly seen them and in this drawing may have been planning a similar series in homage to Schongauer.

The relative inexperience of the young artist is seen here in a certain hesitancy in the drawing of the hands, the awkward foreshortening of the left arm, the disproportionately large head and the incorrect placing of the breasts. It is also apparent in the drawing of legs on the verso, where the muscles do not appear to be securely attached to the bones or tightly enough covered by the skin. Though the two drawings have not the unmatched precision and certainty of Dürer's mature work, they demonstrate his developing mastery of line; the graceful calligraphic patterns of the cascading hair and the flourishes of the garland show his remarkable control of the pen.   L.C.

Baccio Della Porta, called Fra Bartolommeo (1472–1517)

The Sweep of a River with Fishermen and a Town in the Background

Pen and iron gall ink; on white (now stained) laid paper. The sheet unevenly trimmed on all sides, its edges glued to a window mount. The upper left corner torn away and made up, a tear repaired upper left edge. *Maxima*: 20.5 × 29.1

Princes Gate Collection

It was only during the 15th century that Italian painters began to place their figures in convincingly realistic landscape settings, often with perfectly identifiable towns in the background. It is hard to believe that they had not already begun to draw directly from nature as a preparation for such pictures, but there are almost no 15th-century drawings of this kind in existence, Leonardo da Vinci's 1473 pen and ink study of the Arno being a celebrated exception. Nor does the situation notably improve at the start of the 16th century, which only serves to make Fra Bartolommeo's landscape drawings all the more remarkable. Forty-one of them, of which this is one of the outstanding examples, were bequeathed by the artist to his fellow-Dominican and disciple Fra Paolino, and the group remained intact until this century. We cannot know for certain whether Fra Bartolommeo was an especially prolific landscape draughtsman – although we may suspect as much – or whether any number of similar studies by his contemporaries have simply not survived. What is emphatically not in doubt is the sheer freshness and immediacy of these remarkable sheets. The point of the pen is the favourite tool, and proves capable of conjuring up tremendous distances with seemingly effortless economy. In this instance the resulting landscape is spare without being in the least barren, and is drawn in a way that ensures that a definite sense of order is brought to bear on what may at first sight appear to be an entirely spontaneous slice of life. The gently curving motion of the river back to a town in the middle distance is guarded by clumps of trees on either side, while the composition moves from the framing element provided by the rustic building to the left and away to the right. Man takes his place in this convincing but at the same time disciplined environment, while away from all hustle and bustle, a solitary cow grazes peacefully. D.E.

Lorenzo Lotto (c.1480–1556)

Portrait of a Young Man c.1508–10

Black chalk, rubbed in areas with fingertips, heightened with touches of white chalk, and on the lips, red chalk; on white laid paper prepared with a green ground of thin watercolour. A horizontal fold below centre of sheet (top section 19 × 26.9, lower part 14.5 × 26.9 tapering to 26.7), unevenly trimmed, 33.5 × 26.9

Collectors' marks: 'WR' blind stamp, upside down (William Russell: Lugt, 2648); a Lancaster Rose surmounted by a crown (A.G.B. Russell: Lugt, *Suppl.*, 2770a), both lower right.

Princes Gate Collection

This drawing is now generally accepted as an early work by Lorenzo Lotto of c.1508–10, and relates to his painted portraits of that period. The identity of the sitter is unknown.

The artist has used black chalk for the underdrawing, indicating the main outlines of his subject with light, delicate strokes; certain features, such as the nostrils, eyelids, eyesockets, chin and lips, he emphasises with heavier, firm hatchings. Highlights in white chalk appear on the bridge and tip of the nose, and on the sitter's left eyelid, while local colour is suggested by red chalk on the lips. The larger areas of modelling on the cheeks, jowl, and locks of hair hanging below the soft cap on the left side (spectator's right) of the sitter's head, are suggested by broad diagonal strokes, which in some places have been rubbed and washed over by the artist with a brush. In these same areas he appears to have used a denser underlayer of green preparation; this is particularly noticeable on the left cheek, above the upper lip and, to a slightly lesser degree, along the sitter's right jaw. The hair on the right side of the sitter's head has not been indicated, nor does there seem to be any clear evidence of fading in this area, as suggested by Count Seilern in his catalogue (1959).

To modern eyes, the 'unfinished' appearance of the drawing is not disturbing, since the artist has achieved a balanced composition even though he does not even indicate the hair below the brim of the cap on his sitter's right side. The use of a green ground may be derived from silver-point technique, and its use by Lotto in combination with black chalk, should be compared with the much more linear drawing by Hugo van der Goes of *S. Ursula, seated, holding a Book on her Knees*, also in the Princes Gate Collection.

D.F.

129

Michelangelo (1475–1564)

Christ led before Pilate c.1515–20

Preliminary drawing in red chalk for the figures on the left; pen and iron gall ink;
on buff laid paper. A vertical fold, centre, tears repaired lower left corner.
The sheet unevenly trimmed on all sides, and edged by ruled lines in black chalk and iron gall ink,
20.9 × 28.2
A rapid sketch of a man's left leg (iron gall ink), upper centre (*recto*).
Studies of legs and a male torso in red chalk and pen and iron gall ink; inscribed by the artist in pen
and iron gall ink with lines from a sonnet (*verso*).

Collectors' marks 'M' in circle (J.P. Mariette: Lugt, 1852) and '2' lower right;
'RMW' in hexagon (Sir Robert and Lady Witt: Lugt, *Suppl.*, 2228b) lower right on mount.

Princes Gate Collection

The great 18th-century French collector, Mariette, owned this double-sided sheet, and after the dispersal of his collection it seems to have been lost until it reappeared in Sir Robert Witt's collection. Despite its Mariette provenance, the sheet has received only fitful critical attention. For whilst many of the sketches on the *verso* have been accepted universally as Michelangelo's since their publication in 1928 (this side also contains fragments of two sonnets in the artist's hand), the much more important compositional drawing on the *recto* has frequently been written off as the work of a pupil or assistant.

The drawing is certainly autograph. Although compositional studies of this kind are rare in Michelangelo's surviving graphic work, its technique and style can be matched elsewhere. Idiosyncracies such as the claw-like left hand of the figure kneeling in the centre of the composition appear in other drawings; we find this feature in a pen study for *The Crucifixion of Haman* now in the British Museum which was drawn in 1512. The broad slanted hatching strokes reappear in Michelangelo's figurative drawings in pen datable in the 1520s and the way they are used here can be paralleled also in the red chalk compositional drawings of 1515–30. Michelangelo continued to use this technique of hatching (derived from his master Ghirlandaio) in chalk drawings long after he had abandoned pen for figure studies. This drawing also was begun in red chalk. Starting on the left of the sheet, he briefly sketched in chalk the figure of the seated Judge, the kneeling supplicant before him and, more elaborately, the standing female behind the latter. Then he drew over these chalk suggestions in pen and ink, continuing the composition to the right in the same medium.

In the earlier literature, the scene was interpreted as *Christ led before Pilate*. Recently, Tolnay suggested that the episode could represent either S. Lawrence before the Prefect or Christ before Caiaphas, but the earlier suggestion is almost certainly correct, even if the Gospel texts have been treated very freely. The captive figure, long haired and bearded, who is led in is iconographically appropriate as Christ. The type is not that of S. Lawrence. The figure standing behind the kneeling man is the only woman depicted. She turns to address the Judge whilst gesturing toward the prisoner; she is, almost certainly, Pilate's wife, even if her presence is not strictly warranted by any of the Gospel texts. The bearded kneeling man is also clearly important for the narrative, placed in the very foreground plane and, consequently, drawn more heavily (with cross-hatching) than any other figure. His importance has been emphasised for Michelangelo changed the direction of Pilate's gaze so that he gazes down towards this figure. His supplicant pose and almost exaggeratedly coarse features suggest, I believe, that he is the thief Barabas, the prisoner who would be released in place of Christ. All the main participants in the drama have, in other words, been included.

Michelangelo's approach to drawing was essentially utilitarian. Although a ceaseless producer of drawings, they were made, with few exceptions, with a purpose in mind. The ambitious nature of this drawing (there are 12 figures with indications of one or two more)

leaves little doubt that it was made for a specific end. But we have no evidence as to what this was. His pen style remained remarkably consistent and this makes dating difficult; but the sheet is likely to belong to the period of c.1515–20.

Adolfo Venturi, the first critic to recognise that the *recto* is autograph, likened the pen accents to chisel strokes. And it is true that the variety of these strokes, and the large number of changes of direction, are very striking features. What also suggests a relief is the lateral spread of forms and their confinement within a narrow band of depth. It may have been features like these which led Wilde to speculate that the drawing might have been made for one of the reliefs of the unexecuted façade of San Lorenzo (the contracts for the final design dates from 1518). In fact, on a large *modello* of Michelangelo's for the façade (Casa Buonarroti 45A) we find two relief scenes indicated, one a judgement scene which, in this case, does represent S. Lawrence. But nearly 20 reliefs were envisaged for the final elevation and some of these could have been planned to represent scenes from the life of Christ.   M.H.

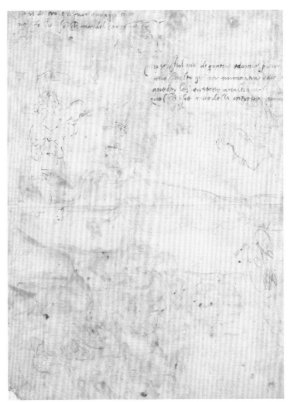

verso

Michelangelo (1475–1564)

The Dream of Human Life c.1533

Black chalk, stippled in the principal figures; on coarse grey laid paper.
The sheet unevenly trimmed on all sides, and torn left and bottom. Backed with paper, laid down on cardboard, 39.6 × 28

Princes Gate Collection

This drawing, as befits its quality, has a distinguished provenance. It belonged to the famous portrait painter, Sir Thomas Lawrence, whose collection of old master drawings was of international repute, including some 100 drawings each by Raphael and Michelangelo. When this drawing was sold by the dealer Samuel Woodburn, Lawrence's executor, in 1836, he described it as coming from the Casa Buonarotti (i.e. Michelangelo's family house), before being owned by J.B.J. Wicar in the 1790s. William Young Ottley acquired it in Italy, and later sold this and many other drawings to Lawrence in 1814. After 1836, it went to William II of Holland's collection, and by 1875 was owned by the Grand Duke of Saxe-Weimar, from whose heir, the Grand Duke Carl Augustus of Saxe-Weimar, it was bought by Count Seilern in 1952.

The late Johannes Wilde wrote of this celebrated drawing that it 'is technically a miracle', and he noted Michelangelo's intention to avoid any kind of linear effect by the extensive use of stippling to denote forms. He dated it to the second half of 1533, but thought it could be a little later, and observed that in this drawing the artist had sought to imitate the shining surface of polished marble and to enhance this effect by contrasting the plasticity of the modelling on the two central figures with the low relief treatment accorded those surrounding them. Such a contrast was characteristic of the new Mannerist style. Kenneth Clark believed that the 'smooth perfection of limb' of the principal figure was derived from Michelangelo's study of antique gems and cameos.

This highly finished work was a 'presentation drawing', either for one of the artist's friends or for a patron, but we do not know for whom it was intended. Nor do we know for certain what the enigmatic subject matter symbolises. It has sometimes been called the *Dream of Michelangelo* or, as here, *The Dream of Human Life*, after the title *Il Sogno* given it by Vasari in 1568, but no contemporary explanations of the allegory survive. Erwin Panofsky, however, recalled the description by Hieronymus Tetius of 1642, which, by its Neoplatonic interpretation would have been in harmony with Michelangelo's general philosophy of life, and Wilde accepted it as a plausible explanation.

In essence, the central figure of the male youth represents the Human Mind which is being re-awakened by the trumpeting angel and reminded of the realm from whence it came. The Neo-Platonists believed the human mind had its real home in the supercelestial sphere, while its life on earth is a dreamlike existence haunted by Vices and illusions (the masks in the open box). The Vices, here represented by six of the Seven Deadly Sins in the surrounding arc of figures, are banished by the trumpeting angel, and the youth brought back from the 'exile' of terrestrial life to celestial virtue.

There are numerous copies after this original drawing, engraved, drawn, and painted, including a painting in the National Gallery, London. The position of the legs and feet of the trumpeting angel has been altered by Michelangelo, and the *pentimenti* are clearly visible in this drawing.   D.F.

Jacopo Carrucci da Pontormo (1494–1556)

Seated Youth c.1525

Black chalk; the principal contours of the figure indented with a stylus; on pale buff laid paper, extensively stained with oil paint. The sheet creased and abraded, particularly on the right, a horizontal fold, centre. Holes repaired lower right side and lower left.
The sheet unevenly trimmed on all sides, vestiges of a ruled line in carbon black ink along top, bottom, and lower left side, 40.5 × 28
Numbered in graphite, upper right: '$\frac{21}{10}$'
Collector's mark, blind stamp 'TL', lower left (Sir Thomas Lawrence: Lugt, 2445).

Study for figure of S. Jerome in red chalk (verso).

Princes Gate Collection

Although this drawing may seem commonplace enough, it is remarkable for its originality, which resides in the fact that it does not appear to be a preparatory study for a more finished work of art such as a painting. (The indentation of the principal contours indicates that it was subsequently reused.) On the other side of the sheet Pontormo has drawn a bald-headed S. Jerome for a picture of the *Madonna with Saints Jerome and Francis*, which is now in the Uffizi. Artists of the previous generation, such as Fra Bartolommeo, Raphael, and even Andrea del Sarto hardly ever seem to have drawn except with the direct intention of using the drawing as a means towards an end. By contrast the drawings of artists of a slightly later generation such as Polidoro da Caravaggio and Parmigianino include a number of depictions of scenes from everyday life. This kind of subject-matter was already customary both in illuminated manuscripts – especially in bas-de-page decorations – and in the backgrounds of pictures, but it does not appear to have been standard in drawings.

Pontormo goes even further. With characteristic intensity he has captured nothing more remarkable than a young boy in workaday clothes, possibly one of the assistants in his shop, sitting with legs uneasily crossed and his right arm resting on a block. His left hand half props up his chin and half covers his face, but fails to conceal the almost haunted look in his eyes. He is doing nothing in particular, and indeed that is the most amazing thing about the drawing. The way in which the figure is brought to life on the paper, with confident strokes of the black chalk and only minor changes of outline, is both powerful and economical, while the setting is simple in the extreme. The sheet probably dates from around 1525, the date of the artist's *Supper at Emmaus*, which was painted for the Certosa (Charterhouse) outside Florence, another masterpiece which manages to combine penetratingly realistic observation with definite emotional disquiet.   D.E.

verso

134

Pieter Bruegel the Elder (c.1525–69)

Landscape with an Artist sketching c.1554–5

Traces of preliminary drawing in graphite; pen and iron gall ink; on pale buff laid paper. The sheet unevenly trimmed on all sides to a ruled line in pen and iron gall ink, 27.7 × 39.6
Inscribed in pen and iron gall ink, in a 16th-century hand lower left: 'de ouden Bruegel'; and in an old hand in graphite, *verso*: 'der oude Breugel na 56'

Princes Gate Collection

Executed c.1554–5 probably in the studio after Bruegel's journey to and from Italy across the Alps, this drawing is one of several similar views. Some of these were preliminary to the engraved *Large Landscape* series, printed and published by Hieronymous Cock in 1556 and others, like this, were completed compositions. One of Bruegel's earliest biographers, Carel van Mander, in his *Het Schilderboeck* of 1604 wrote:

> 'Pieter painted many pictures from life as he travelled about, so that it was said of him, that while visiting the Alps, he had swallowed all the mountains and cliffs, and, upon coming home, he had spat them forth upon his canvases and panels; so remarkably was he able to follow these and other works of nature.'

The drawing, although meticulous in its rendering of the detail of nature may not be a completely literal transcription of a place in the Alps but more as van Mander suggests, an accumulation of his experiences there. It is known that he used chalk studies to aid his memory and therefore he at least spent some time sketching in the open air as the artist in the scene is doing. An artist seen sketching outside with the book on his lap was not an uncommon motif in pictures, derived from the Italians. There is a painting in the National Gallery, London, by an anonymous Netherlandish master of c.1530/40 and an etching by Hoefnagel of a landscape with Mercury and Psyche as the subject after a drawing by Bruegel himself of 1553 which also show artists. These pictures reflect a change in attitude from the imaginary scenes to a more naturalistic rendering of landscape with took place in the 16th century. This was part of a wider appreciation of landscape as a subject worthy of being painted and drawn in its own right. There are faint traces of graphite on this drawing which suggests that the outlying composition was sketched on the spot and further elaborated upon at home in ink.

Instead of a large tree, a huge craggy rock on the right acts as the *repoussoir* bringing one straight into the scene. This was a conventional compositional device at this time. The wild, romantic shapes of the mountains and trees are an exaggerated form of the artist's response to the landscape as well as showing an influence of Italian artists such as Muziano, Titian and Campagnola, whose work he may have seen in Italy or from engravings after them. However, the vigorous play of fine little strokes over pale buff, without wash, which gives a three-dimensional quality to the trees and rocks and an effect of light and air to the whole scene is his own technique which he used in a more restrained manner in his painting.   T.J.

136

Pieter Bruegel the Elder (c.1525–69)

Kermesse at Hoboken 1559

Traces of preliminary drawing in black chalk; pen and iron gall ink; on pale buff laid paper (watermark: crossed arrows). The sheet abraded in the area of the ring of dancers, the most distant figures of which retouched in black chalk. Unevenly trimmed on all sides, apparently to a ruled line in graphite (partly visible top and bottom). Vertical and horizontal folds, centre. Pressed through for engraving, with vestiges of preparation with black chalk, *verso*, 26.5 × 39.4

Signed and dated in pen and brown ink, lower left: '1559/BRVEGEL', and inscribed by the artist on the banner, left: 'Gilde/.../hoboken/.../.../...'

Lee Collection

A kermesse is a fair; Hoboken, then a village south west of Antwerp, is now a suburb of that city. Bruegel's drawing shows the village, identified by the inscription on the banner, much as it must have appeared in 1559. The buildings on the left and right are inns, the 'Horn' and the 'Fleur-de-Lys'; the village church is in the centre; behind the churchyard is a mansion, the residence of Melchior Schetz, who was a successful Antwerp banker and who in 1559 bought, from two different sellers, the mansion and lordship of Hoboken. Fairs were held at Hoboken early in May and in September. Bruegel has here represented the Whitsuntide festival of the Hoboken Guild of Longbowmen, whose banner is displayed on the left and some of whom are shooting at the target on the right. Crossbowmen appear in the procession which conducts the image of a Saint into the church and pilgrims are being received at the inn of the 'Fleur-de-Lys'. It is not quite clear what the holiday attractions may be which are at the centres of the two groups of villagers in the background. The foreground cart appears to be a mobile brothel; beneath a tree two lovers embrace lustily. The central dance may be a children's game, with two bagpipers providing the music, but villagers emerging from the inn on the left are also dancing. Bruegel has compressed into this small sheet all the activities of a village holiday. In the same year he painted two of his great encyclopaedic pictures: *The Fight between Carnival and Lent* (Vienna) and the village populated by *The Netherlandish Proverbs* (Berlin), in both of which he described an endless variety of human behaviour.

This drawing, a design for a print, was engraved by Frans Hogenberg and published by Bartholomeus de Momper, who was not Bruegel's usual publisher but who in 1559 issued a second *Peasant Kermesse* engraving by another artist. The print after Bruegel's drawing is inscribed: 'Those peasants rejoice at such festivals/Dancing, leaping, drinking themselves stupid like beasts/They must keep up those kermesses/Even if they should starve or die of over-eating' (literally, 'of chewing': the word is chosen to preserve the rhyme scheme). The lines were supplied by the publisher, who attached similar verses to the second *Kermesse* print which he issued. They need not bear any relation to Bruegel's own opinions of village life.   L.C.

Pieter Bruegel the Elder (c.1525–69)

View of Antwerp from the Sea c.1559

Preliminary drawing in graphite underlying boats, gallows and town; pen and iron gall ink on buff laid paper. The lower left corner torn away and made up. The sheet edged with a ruled line in pen and iron gall ink on left, 20 × 30

Inscribed, lower left, in a 19th-century hand in iron gall ink: 'Breughel' (within an oval outline)

Princes Gate Collection

Unlike most of Bruegel's drawings this is of an actual place, even if it is a distant view. It is of Antwerp where he became a master of the guild of painters in 1551 and where he lived, apart from his stay in Italy, until 1563. The date of this drawing is c.1559. The more considered presence of cross-hatched pen lines especially within the large waves in the foreground creates a stronger sense of violence and supports this date. It is a development from the tame application of ink in the alpine studies.

During the 1550s there was a shift among artists such as Herri met de Bles and Bruegel's printer Hieronymous Cock, from the representation of calm sea views framed by landscapes of rugged rocks or clearly defined towns to stormy seas with only a faint outline of land in the distance. An extreme example in Bruegel's work is a painting, *Storm at Sea* (Kunsthistorisches Museum, Vienna), thought to be one of his last pictures where sea and sky are shown as fully integrated elements. The dramatic storm became a popular subject for artists in 17th-century Holland and then in England during the 18th and 19th centuries.

In this drawing the sea is emphasised rather than the city. The interest in the sea reflects the growing dependence of the Low Countries on it for trade and commerce as well as diplomacy. Bruegel's work is innovative and unusual for this time because there is no land in the foreground and two-thirds of the space is taken up with sea. It is very close to a pure seascape. Although the landscape in the background is only just recognisable, for the architectural details are barely visible, he shows himself more willing to experiment with new ideas in his drawings than he does in his paintings.

Bruegel uses long strokes of the pen close together or crossed to conjure up the feeling of waves being whipped up by the wind. The effect of even longer straight parallel lines bursting forth from the clouds on the upper right to suggest heavy rainfall is bold, and the presence of the wind is also suggested by the angle of the sailing boat right of centre which leans dangerously low. The form of swirling waves and foamy crests had been explored in detail by Leonardo da Vinci. Bruegel creates a pattern of crested peaks and thus a feeling of movement in the rising and falling of the water that may be less scientific and less like curls of hair, as in a Leonardo drawing, but still seems realistic.

The gallows on the sandbank are no doubt pure invention, a portentous reminder of death and retribution. All the vessels appear to be heading out to sea, where there is obviously a storm, away from the sunshine and safety of the harbour. T.J.

Sir Peter Paul Rubens (1577–1640)

Study of a Wild Cherry Tree with Brambles and Weeds c.1620

Black chalk, with some red chalk for the flowers and berries, lower centre, and touches of
synthetic yellow chalk, apparently applied moistened; traces of heightening in white chalk;
on coarse grey-buff (now extensively stained and foxed) recycled laid paper. Horizontal folds,
centre of sheet, where the drawing is abraded and disturbed. The bottom right corner torn away,
the sheet unevenly trimmed on all sides, and laid down. *Maxima*: 54.6 × 49.6
Twelve inscriptions by the artist in black chalk noting principally the colours of the plants.

Princes Gate Collection

This drawing of a wild cherry tree with ivy or
briony and a vine at the side is one of a small
number of plant and foliage studies in Rubens'
work: other examples are in the British Museum,
the Louvre, and Chatsworth. Of these, only the
Louvre sheet can be securely connected with a
painting, *The Wild Boar Hunt* in Dresden, usually
dated 1615–20.

A.E. Popham's suggestion that this drawing
may be related to the painting *An Autumn
Landscape with a View of Het Steen* of 1636 (National
Gallery, London) received support from Count
Seilern, who observed that the Helicampene
plant shown here (but otherwise rare in Rubens'
landscapes) also appears in the National
Gallery's picture – a claim not substantiated by a
botanical expert. Seilern also dated the sheet to
the 1630s on stylistic grounds, yet it has little in
common with either the composition or handling
of the atmospheric drawings of distant fields,
water, and lines of trees which are normally
assigned to this period of Rubens' career.

Julius Held perceived a relationship between
this drawing, that in the Louvre mentioned
above, and a *Study of a Tree Trunk and Brambles* at
Chatsworth. Both Louvre and Chatsworth compositions, drawn in ink above preliminary chalk
work, are created by a similar process, at each
stage of which a comparable handling is evident.
The strong tonal contrasts established in these

compositions are beyond the range of the delicate chalk notations of the present work, yet
the disparate treatment of forms visible here
may nevertheless be equated with that in the
two stages of evolution of those drawings. For
example, the ovals, scallops and areas of hooked
strokes which denote leaf clusters and shadow at
the centre of this sheet are clearly associated with
the formal vocabulary of the preliminary drawing of both sheets cited above. The patches of
shadow at the bottom of this drawing are created
from tight zigzags, against which the form of the
bramble's stem and leaves are redefined and
silhouetted by a dark, sharp chalk line: and the
process of clarification of form and polarisation of
tones, and the intensity and precision of strokes
by which this is here accomplished, relate to the
stage of pen overdrawing in the Louvre and
Chatsworth compositions.

The composition of this drawing, in which
cherry tree and brambles form a diagonal across
the page, may also be seen as a reversal of that in
the Chatsworth work. Since the drawing shows
variants of a motif included in paintings by
Rubens executed as early as c.1617 (e.g. *The
Watering Place*, National Gallery, London) and
has stylistic and formal affinities with sheets
datable to c.1620, a similarly early date may
perhaps now be assigned to it.   W.B.

Sir Peter Paul Rubens (1577–1640)

Helena Fourment c.1630

Black and red chalk heightened with white. Pen and iron gall ink in the headdress and in some details of the head, possibly including later retouchings. On white, now discoloured, laid paper; the figure has been cut round in silhouette and backed, on coarser laid paper tinted with greyish-buff wash, 61.2 × 55

Princes Gate Collection

Helena Fourment (1614–73) was Rubens' second wife; his first wife, Isabella Brant (1591–1626) whom he married in October 1609, had been dead for four years when he married Helena at Antwerp on 6 December 1630. She was the daughter of an Antwerp silk and tapestry merchant Daniel Fourment, and his wife, Clara Stappaert. He had four children by his first marriage and five by his second, the last born just over eight months after his death. A portrait of Helena's elder sister, Susanna, is in the National Gallery, London.

This portrait probably dates from shortly after Helena's marriage to Rubens, and she appears to be dressed for church and is holding a prayer-book with a gloved hand. With her bare right hand she draws back the 'huke' or 'heuke', a fashionable, all-enveloping garment which was suspended from a tasselled skull cap and reached to the ground, protecting the wearer from wind and rain.

The sheet is among Rubens' most splendid drawings, being quite exceptional in its scale and its rich and elaborate technique. Despite having been cut round and sustaining some damage in, for example, the area of the sitter's forehead, it is still remarkably fresh and sparkling. So far as is known, the drawing is not a preparatory study for a painting, but an independent work of art of great charm. It clearly had a very special significance for the artist, which is reflected in his spirited but tender treatment of this portrait of his young bride. D.F.

Sir Anthony van Dyck (1599–1641)

Figure of a Man bending forward c.1617

Black chalk, with traces of heightening with white chalk, probably applied with a moist brush for all motifs except the hand, extreme right; charcoal (?) in the hand, right; on pale buff laid paper. The sheet unevenly trimmed on all sides and laid down, apparently on the mount of Jonathan Richardson the Elder. *Maxima*: 27 × 43.15

Inscribed in pen and iron gall ink, lower right by a later hand: 'Van Dyck' Collectors' marks: P.H. Lankrink, lower right centre (Lugt, 2090); and J. Richardson the Elder, lower right (Lugt, 2183). Also inscribed by Richardson in pen and iron gall ink on *verso* of mount with shelf and box numbers: '10.44./GG.10./Y.22/Z.'

Witt Collection

This is a study from life for the figure pulling at Christ's garment in one of van Dyck's earliest works, *The Carrying of the Cross* in S. Paul's, Antwerp. The painting is one of a series of 15, still in the church, showing the Mysteries of the Rosary commissioned by the Antwerp Dominicans from several Flemish artists, among them Rubens, Jordaens, Cornelis de Vos, and Hendrick van Balen (van Dyck's master). The date of the painting and therefore also this drawing is c.1617, since one of the Rubens paintings is so dated. The commission was early in van Dyck's career, before he went to Italy and even before he became a master at the Antwerp guild of painters in 1618.

Although the finished picture, whilst showing the influence of Rubens and Jordaens, is still a little unsatisfactory because of the rather awkward crowding, one can see from this drawing how the young van Dyck was beginning to master human form. The arm in the middle of the three on the left and the faint hand on the extreme right were the positions he finally used. In the drawing the model, by leaning on his left knee and grasping an object tightly in his right hand with an outstretched arm, recreates the posture in the artist's imagination. Van Dyck was obviously concerned to simulate the tension, shown in the strong contours around the arms and the modulation of light over the muscular surface. Such a detailed drawing as this would be the last stage of preparation before painting. Using the method of the Italian Renaissance and contemporary artists, van Dyck would have already drawn several of the related studies of the overall composition, most of which survive, and possibly the larger compositional drawing, the *modello* with squared grid lines for its transfer on to canvas (Stedelijk Prentenkabinet, Antwerp).

Two collectors' marks may be seen on the drawing, one in the right hand corner and the other below the knee of the figure. One belongs to Prosper Henry Lankrink, the other to Jonathan Richardson Snr., whose collection the artist Antoine Watteau may have seen when he came to London in 1719. This has been suggested because its influence can be seen in the similar type of study by Watteau for his painting *Jupiter and Antiope*, in the Louvre, Paris. It is more likely, however, that Watteau, who originally came from Flanders, saw van Dyck's painting in Antwerp.   T.J.

Francesco Barbieri, called Guercino (1591–1666)

Aurora 1621

Red chalk with some slight rubbing; on pale grey (stained and discoloured) laid paper. The sheet creased, lower right corner, and unevenly trimmed on all sides, 24.85 × 27.2
Numbered in graphite, upper left (now largely effaced): '48'

Witt Collection

This drawing was made in Rome during the summer of 1621 in preparation for a frescoed ceiling in a Garden Pavilion belonging to the Papal nephew Cardinal Ludovico Ludovisi. The subject, Aurora (Dawn), drives her chariot across the sky to free the world from darkness. This was a vital commission with which Guercino made his Roman début. Though beautiful the drawing was impracticable, for on the ceiling Aurora required steeper foreshortening and a greater sense of physical and psychological distance. The direction was reversed in favour of a more easily legible passage from left to right. Here we still feel the presence of the posed model but on the wall Aurora looks upwards not outwards and more like an ecstatic Saint than a draped domestic, the gesture of whose flower-scattering hand is easily mistaken for a friendly wave.

Inspired by Correggio, Guercino exploits the colour and texture of red chalk. Characteristic of his distinctive graphic style is the uneven emphasis on separated points of interest, the delicate rubbed transitions from light to dark, the shadowed eyes and the variety in the force, width, and direction of strokes which range from the tentatively corrected contour of the arm to the calligraphic flourish of the sleeve over the chariot. The chalk picks up the grain of the paper which is coarser than that which Guercino uses when working with pen and ink. The central accent on the heavy hand whose projection is artificially promoted by the over-emphatic surrounding shading is often found in his pictures.

In life Dawn may be pink or white skylight; in Latin poetry a 'rosy fingered' maiden. In Art Guercino employs the classical imagery familiar to his cultured patron; he also follows his own preference for broken surfaces, and across the page uses movement, whose direction coincides with the fall of flickering light, to bring Dawn to our sight through stumped *sfumato* in a rich flush of deep red chalk.

Guercino treasured his own drawings and resisted offers from collectors. He took this one back home to Cento in 1623 and to Bologna when he moved house in 1643. Guercino was dedicated to teaching through drawing. He illustrated an instructional manual for beginners and he organised local life classes. This drawing formed part of the study collection which he left to his nephews Benedetto and Cesare Gennari whom he had trained as painters.

J.F.

Jusepe de Ribera (1591–1652)

A Man tied to a Tree late 1620s

Red chalk; on off-white laid paper. The sheet made up at each corner, extensively repaired and cleaned, 24.1 × 15.1
Inscribed in an old hand in pen and iron gall ink, bottom left: 'Spagnoletto'
Witt Collection

Ribera made a number of drawings at different moments in his career of the motif of the man tied to the tree: of these, probably the earliest is a red chalk study of *S. Albert* (British Museum) signed and dated 1626. This sheet, in which the figure is defined by sharp, continuous contours and dense, precise interior hatching, presents an example of Ribera's early 'academic' manner of draughtsmanship.

The present sheet may be assigned a date later in the 1620s. Here, the elegant body of S. Bartholomew (whose elongated fingers, arms and legs are typical of Ribera's treatment of certain figure types) is rendered by contours which, in contrast to those in the drawing mentioned above, vary in sharpness, accent and weight. The boundaries of forms eroded by light are now suggested by the faintest of broken lines, which contrast with the firm, continuous stroke indicating the volume of a limb in shadow. In shaded areas, occasional strokes are particularly heavily accented, amplifying the gamut of tonal variation in the contour. Compatible with the spare, but richly modulated outlines is the reticent interior modelling: the structure of the rib cage is suggested by sparse, curved hatching, but a reading of other planes of the torso relies on accents such as those denoting nipple and navel. Some of the subtlety of drawing in the body emanates to adjacent areas of the tree. For example, the curved strokes over the trunk, economical indications of volume and cast shadow, also echo the line of the Saint's buttock and leg, thereby securing the placing of the figure on the sheet. Such drawing effects a transition between the handling of the nude and the loose execution of landscape elements. The relationship of Saint and tree is further consolidated by analogies of form: for the branch at the left mirrors Bartholomew's gesturing right arm.

Behind the tree is the figure of a second man, which is in every detail the antithesis of that of the Saint. He is clothed, seated in shadow in a cramped posture, back turned towards the drawing's principal motif. Rapidly silhouetted by a continuous, uniformly thick contour, the figure's interior modelling is supplanted by overall parallel hatching, which denies volume. The lumpy form of the figure's back, however, coarsely echoes the suave curve of the Saint's body from right armpit to knee. Similar juxtapositions of hunched, draped figures with fully extended nudes occur in a drawing in Princeton (sketchier than the present work, but of similar date) and in a pen drawing of a torture scene of 1635–37 (Teylers Museum, Haarlem).

The handling of the present drawing is closely comparable with that in a study of S. Sebastian in the Gere Coll., London, and in sketches for the figure of Cain, in Florence. W.B.

Spagnoletto

Jan van Goyen (1596–1656)

Landscape with Oak Tree 1630s

Black chalk; brush and carbon black ink washes; on off-white laid paper.
The pictorial area enclosed by a ruled line in pen and iron gall ink.
The sheet unevenly trimmed at all sides, 13 × 15.9

Witt Collection

This drawing, datable to the 1630s, is of a format unique within van Goyen's *oeuvre*, in that it is almost square. The format employed by the artist for paintings in which a single tree predominates (of which examples in Philadelphia, Prague and London are dated 1633) is vertical, while other drawings treating this subject are clearly horizontal. It is in the drawings, rather than in paintings, that van Goyen seems to have felt at liberty to experiment with the motif of the solitary, dominant tree without the inclusion of picturesque staffage, such as birdhunters, shepherds or washerwomen.

The oak in this drawing is rendered by a dense network of nervous hooked and curling strokes, comparable to those describing the tree in a sheet in the Ames Coll., New London, also datable to the 1630s. Unlike the Ames drawing, the example reproduced here is overlayed by a series of finely gradated carbon ink washes which extends the composition's tonal range and subtlety: the practice of applying grey washes was to become habitual in van Goyen's drawings only in 1647. The degree of realisation and refinement visible in this sheet suggests that, despite its lack of signature, it was conceived as a completed work of art in its own right.

In both this and the Ames drawing, the powerful diagonal thrust of the tree trunk is counterbalanced by a gently sloping terrain controlled by a low horizon-line. However, the oak in this design, in contrast to that in the New London sheet, is cropped at the upper and lower edges of the pictorial area, thus bringing the motif closer to the spectator and enhancing its immediacy. An experiment with a similar composition is seen in the rapid chalk study of a tree, probably on a page from a sketchbook, in the Oehler Coll., Kassel. In that work, which is, however, horizontal in format, van Goyen explores a pictorial structure similar to that visible here (although the tree leans in the opposite direction) but the sheet does not appear to have been trimmed at the edges. The present drawing, by contrast, seems to have been deliberately cut by the artist in order to maximise the impact of the dominant diagonal design. The composition may have been trimmed from a sheet measuring 17 × 27cm., the larger of two sketchbook sizes favoured by van Goyen when creating formal, finished drawings.
W.B.

Rembrandt van Rijn (1606–69)

Study of Seated Actor c.1635

Pen and iron gall ink; brush and iron gall ink wash; on pale buff laid paper.
The sheet trimmed on all sides, and edged with a ruled line in pen and iron gall ink,
18.5 × 14.4
A study of the head of the same actor, in pen and iron gall ink (*verso*).
Collector's mark, lower left, of E. Bouverie (Lugt, 325).

Princes Gate Collection

This lively drawing is a characteristic example of Rembrandt's drawing style c.1635. Even though the subject is seated there is a great sense of movement conveyed by the most rapid use of the pen. A multitude of short lines are scattered haphazardly and there are longer lines which sweep smoothly over the surface. All are made with a quill pen which in the hands of a master can produce sharply-defined lines, which here end in a little curl. The actor may have been posing but one has the impression, on the contrary, that Rembrandt has captured a fleeting moment. It was at this time that one could say Rembrandt came closest to the 'Baroque' manner.

Throughout his life he had close contacts with the theatre whether it was with Vondel, the Dutch playwright whose plays were performed at the Amsterdam theatre which opened in 1638, or the travelling actors, some of whom were from England, who performed *commedia dell'arte* and were seen at fairs. Theatre for Rembrandt was yet another scene from everyday life. There are many examples of his illustrations of actors particularly among his drawings. There is a group of drawings of about 1637–8 that are close in style to each other, some showing a bishop and others a woman richly dressed (previously called the *Jewish Bride*) which may be related to Vondel's play *Gijsbrecht von Aemstel* that was performed in 1638. More recently some of the subjects of his paintings have also been related to scenes in plays.

The plumed hat, tassled and embroidered cloak, large boots and walking stick of the actor in our drawing is a characteristic costume for comedy actors of the period and cannot be related to any particular play. There are also

verso

several drawings by Rembrandt where it is clear that the actors are on a stage; in one someone is seen below clapping. Here, it is impossible to tell, except that his face has a more attentive expression than one would imagine if he were relaxing offstage. On the *verso* is the same head with a more solemn look. Rembrandt obviously made more than one attempt at capturing the expression. It is also very close to a drawing where a similarly dressed figure talks to a kneeling man (Rijksprentenkabinet, Amsterdam), which at least suggests they are rehearsing. T.J.

Rembrandt van Rijn (1606–69)

A Quack addressing a Crowd at a Fair c.1637–40

Pen (reed used for foreground figures of mother and baby) and iron gall ink;
brush and iron gall ink wash, with some drawing with the flat of the brush, and
some use of the dry brush; white bodycolour, mixing with ink wash in the
quack's banner, and used as a corrective over foreground mother and child; on
off-white laid paper. The sheet unevenly trimmed on all sides, and edged with a
ruled line in pen and iron gall ink. Tears repaired, upper right corner and right
edge, 18.8 × 16.65
Numbered (by the artist?), in iron gall ink, lower right centre: '2'
Collector's mark: Friedrich August II of Saxony, lower right (Lugt, 971).

Princes Gate Collection

Rembrandt was particularly successful at rendering the reality of Dutch life in the
17th century in his drawings. Very few were preliminary drawings for a specific
composition, whether to be painted or etched. He had no particular method nor
was there any real distinction between different types of drawing. Some sketches
were drawn from nature, particularly his landscapes, and others were from his
imagination, but the scene would be as real as if it were from nature as in this
drawing. It may be dated to about 1637–40. The composition is firmly delineated
with strong vertical and horizontal lines drawn in long continuous strokes. The
angular forms are strongly outlined with a reed pen which produces different
thicknesses within one line and sometimes even cuts into the paper, as has
happened with the execution of the large seated woman and child in the
immediate foreground. He used this type of pen more frequently from the late
1630s. The forms are also more solid with a heavier application of wash than those
in the *Seated Actor*. The tones are darker in the foreground getting lighter as the
scene recedes. Different shades or gradations were also applied to emphasize the
shadow, a technique which has similarities to his painting style.

The 1630s were a prosperous time for Rembrandt. He was well established in
Amsterdam with a wife, house, studio and plenty of patrons. The design of the
composition shows confidence, and has been contrived.The curve of the crowd
reflects the curve of the umbrella above, and is balanced by the triangular shape of
the sign on the right. It is therefore unlikely that Rembrandt was sitting in the
street sketching the scene. The viewpoint, taken from behind the subject, is
characteristic of Rembrandt who used it several times, as, for example, in the
famous etching, *The Raising of Lazarus* of 1632.

Quacks were a familiar sight at markets and fairs at this time and were often
depicted by Dutch genre artists with their large signs, Chinese umbrellas, holding
forth to their gullible customers. Rembrandt himself had etched and drawn this
subject before (a related drawing is in the Print Room, Berlin). Ironically it is a
scene closer to the theatre, especially in the light of recent scientific advances that
had been made in the field of medicine in the 17th century. Rembrandt's quack
looks more like a character in a play: he stands above the audience as if on a stage,
clad in fanciful attire, with a funny tall hat, sweeping cloak and a bird on his
shoulders. We see the scene as if, like the artist, we are in the wings of a theatre,
remote from the audience yet able to view all that is happening on stage.   T.J.

Alonso Cano (1601–67)

Studies for an Annunciation (recto) 1652–5
Study for the Madonna and Child (verso)

Pen and iron gall ink, with some use of either the dry brush or fingers (*recto*);
pen and iron gall ink (*verso*); on off-white laid paper, 37.4 × 21.8
Witt Collection

The studies on the *recto*, datable to 1652–55, relate to Cano's painting of *The Annunciation* in Granada Cathedral. The composition shown here was substantially revised in the painting, which was designed to be hung 25 metres above floor-level. Three principal stages of the composition's evolution may be defined in the drawing, despite the obscuring of some preliminary penwork by later hatching. Initially, the Virgin grasped the narrow curtain which descended from swags and clusters of fruit, right, pulling it protectively across her back. The curtain was then extended to rise at the left, and a putto introduced to support it. Below the putto, smudged ink masks the conjunction of contours of the original curtain with those of the later addition, while smudges to the left of the cherub efface the extended curtain's edge. Finally, the upper corners of the curtain were connected by a shallow arc, creating above the Virgin's head a canopy, supported from high in the right of the composition by a second putto, whose form remains unresolved. The flying cherub at the top of the sheet was probably invented at this stage: this figure, together with the putto at the left of the prayer-desk, reappears in a graphite study of c.1645–1657 (Biblioteca Nacional, Madrid).

The cherub by the prayer-desk is ambiguous, and may be interpreted either as a motif of ornamental sculpture (similar to those created by Cano himself) or as a celestial being. A different type of ambiguity, retained perhaps to indicate possibilities for the final composition, is seen in the Virgin's head: *pentimenti* here encourage alternative readings of the form as either turning towards the prayer-desk, or inclining towards the right, an area occupied in the painted composition by the Archangel Gabriel. Minor *pentimenti* occur in the putto at the upper left, although outlines describing the right side of this figure, and of that of the Virgin, are constantly qualified by short strokes which accentuate the plasticity of

verso

the forms. The bold simplification of contours and emphatic marking of planes in the Virgin's body may be compared to the treatment of the reclining nude in the sketch of c.1648–52 (Feduchi Coll., Madrid). The putto at the lower left of this sheet – the first of this rhythmically related group to be drawn – combines the poses of the two cherubs above. Variants of the putti stated here at the centre and right appear at the upper left and right, respectively, of the painting.

The sketch on the *verso* of the sheet, stylistically related to the drawing of the putto on the right, *recto*, is almost certainly a study for a Madonna of the Rosary. However, it is not related to the only painting of this subject extant in Cano's work.

Gianlorenzo Bernini (1598–1680)

The Louvre, East Façade (first project)

Traces of preliminary constructional indentations with ruler and stylus; pen and iron gall ink; on thin buff laid paper. The sheet laid down, with blue facing paper overlaying the backing sheet, and obscuring the edges of the drawing, 16.4 × 27.7 (sight measurements)
Inscribed on *recto*: 'Cav Bernini No 42 110v'; and on *verso*: 'Cav Bernino'.

Blunt Collection

The appointment of Jean Baptiste Colbert as *Surintendant des Bâtiments* in January 1664 was radically to alter the history of the Louvre. The completion of the palace and in particular the main east façade had been entrusted to Louis Le Vau and work had begun in 1661. He was now summarily dismissed and Colbert set about obtaining projects from other leading French architects such as François Mansart. But failing to find any that he deemed suitable he turned to Italy. Using Abbé Elpidio Benedetti as his emissary he solicited projects from among others Gianlorenzo Bernini. The Italian master complied and sent his first of what turned out to be four projects for the building to Paris.

That the project is italianate in character (e.g. flat rather than steeply pitched roofs) should not be surprising. Bernini had not, at this stage, ever travelled to France and so his knowledge of French architecture must have been limited. Also, his chauvinism toward the French and their art when he did, in fact, go to Paris suggests the improbability of him catering to French taste. Consequently the spatial complexity of the curvilinear façade with its convex central core framed by concave wings depends more upon contemporary ideas for façade design in Rome, such as Borromini's S. Carlino or his own S. Andrea Quirinale, than upon derivative schemes to be seen in Paris like Le Vau's Collège des Quatre Nations.

A palace for the most powerful monarch in Europe, Louis XIV, required an architectural vocabulary to match. Bernini strongly criticized Le Vau's scheme with its superimposed orders as being more appropriate for 'a wooden cabinet' than a royal palace and replaced them with a giant order of half columns linking the two storeys. He also altered the character of the façade giving it an open two-storey arcade more commonly associated in Italy with public or government buildings than with private dwellings. For his models he had turned to some of the most impressive buildings of the preceding century. The giant order recalls those of Michelangelo's S. Peter's and Palladio's Loggia del Capitaniato in Vicenza, while the arcading with a Palladian motif above an arch follows that of Sansovino's Library of S. Mark in Venice. The unusual domeless drum rising through the middle of the building has, by contrast, few precedents; the lilies that decorate the skyline give it the appearance of a crown, an association certainly made by Colbert himself.

Bernini's project, although conceived on a scale which would certainly have appealed to the Sun King, neglected the requirements of a palace intended to house the court and, of course, Louis XIV himself. It was, as a result, rejected.

P.D.

Cav. Bernini N.º 42   110·½

Sir Peter Lely (1618–80)

Two Heralds in Ceremonial Dress mid-1660s

Black chalk, with white chalk applied both dry and with a moist brush as heightening, and as a corrective on the herald, right; charcoal(?) with heightening in white chalk applied with the brush, and some redrawing in black chalk for the figure on the left; on blue (discoloured) laid paper. The principal, irregularly-shaped sheet made up by the artist with additions on the left, top, and right. The drawing unevenly trimmed on all sides, to a ruled line in pen and carbon black ink. *Maxima*: 51.8 × 36.4
Collector's mark: 'RMW' in hexagon, lower left (Sir Robert and Lady Witt: Lugt, *Suppl.*, 2228 b)

Witt Collection

Thirty-one drawings survive from a series of large figure studies made by Lely of the Procession of the Order of the Garter, which took place – and still takes place – annually on S. George's Day, 23 April.

Charles I had been an enthusiastic promoter of the Order and its ceremonies, and one of the ways in which after the Restoration Charles II emphasized the continuity of the monarchy was to revive the College and Chapter of the Order and to carry out its ceremonies with full splendour. Garter processions are known to have taken place at Whitehall in 1667 and 1671, and may have been staged in other years. The vividness of Lely's drawings suggest that he had witnessed such a ceremony. However, he also owned the oil sketch of a Garter procession made by van Dyck, probably in 1638, in which figures quite similar in style and mood are indicated. Lely's highly finished drawings may have been intended as ends in themselves, rather than as preparatory studies for some large scale work such as the set of tapestries which van Dyck is reported to have had in view.

Lely shows the figures walking slowly from right to left, conversing and gesturing to one another, the poor knights, canons and heralds (as here) in pairs, the pursuivants, the senior officers of the Order, and the garter knights themselves, singly. Several individuals can be identified and it has been suggested that the two intended to be represented in this drawing are Thomas St George, Somerset Herald, and John Wingfield, York Herald. One may speculate that one of the heads remains unfinished because Lely had not yet been able to take the likeness of Mr. St George.

Sir Oliver Millar dates the drawings to the mid-1660s, when the artist was at the height of his powers, and describes them as 'the most powerfully baroque drawings ever produced in England'. J.A.N.

Claude Gellée, called Claude Lorrain (1600–82)

Study for 'Landscape with the Landing of Aeneas in Latium' 1673

Preliminary drawing in graphite; pen and iron gall ink; brush and iron gall ink wash and iron gall mixed with carbon black; white chalk applied as bodycolour with a moist brush, used as both heightening and corrective; traces of black chalk; on thin off-white laid paper. The pictorial area enclosed by ruled and freehand lines in graphite and iron gall ink. The sheet unevenly trimmed on all sides. *Maxima*: 18.4 × 25.35
Signed and dated in iron gall ink, bottom left: 'Roma 1675 [?] Claude fecit', with the artist's inscriptions in ink (now partly effaced) upper left and right.

Princes Gate Collection

One of seven extant preliminary drawings for the painting *Landscape with the Landing of Aeneas*, dated 1675, this work may be assigned to early 1673, although it was later inscribed by Claude '1675'(?). The subject is taken from the *Aeneid*, Book VIII, in which Virgil describes the meeting between Aeneas and Pallas, son of Evander, king of the city of Pallanteum. Having reached the mouth of the Tiber as war erupted in Latium, Aeneas was advised by the river god to ally his forces with Evander's. He duly crewed two biremes, and rowing upstream, arrived at Pallanteum, the future site of Rome, as Evander and his retinue were offering sacrifices in a nearby wood. Seeing foreign vessels, Pallas armed himself to meet them. He was greeted from the stern of one of the boats by Aeneas, who, proffering an olive branch, asked for friendship.

The painting was commissioned by Don Gaspare Altieri as a pendant to a work which Claude had painted in 1622 for Altieri's father, Angelo Albertoni. Don Gaspare also prescribed the picture's subject matter: significantly, his wife's family, whose name he had acquired and to whom his political prominence was indebted, claimed descent from Aeneas, a connection which Claude acknowledged in the painting by adding the Altieri arms to a flag on Aeneas' boats.

The earliest preparatory drawings, dating from 1672, show in the right foreground Aeneas greeting Pallas from one of the vessels close to shore. At the left, Pallanteum's wooded slopes are screened by two foreground clumps of vertical trees: each clump also contains one diagonal trunk.

In the present sheet, by contrast, Claude reduces the significance of Aeneas' encounter with Pallas by setting it in the middleground of a landscape expanded both in depth and width. An extensive *repoussoir* hillock now occupies the foreground, while at the right are ruined citadels beyond which rise two hills. In this extended landscape, the artist alludes for the first time to later moments in Virgil's narrative; four inscriptions identify the citadels as Janiculum and Saturnia, which Evander pointed out to Aeneas after entering Pallanteum. The hill at the left is similarly identified as the Aventine, where the monster Cacus, of whose tyranny Aeneas also learned at Pallanteum, formerly had his lair.

The number of trees in the early sketches is here reduced. The foreground clumps are supplanted by a single diagonal trunk which dominates the composition's extreme left quarter, framing the view of a distant estuary – a majestic formal element which appears in no other preparatory drawing for the painting. Aeneas' boats, initially drawn close to the shore, were effaced (although their masts remain visible) and repositioned in the middle of the river, to the right of the composition's central axis, thus creating a more evenly balanced design.

The ruled horizontal, vertical and diagonal grid which divides the completed composition into quarters was not an aid for transferring the design to canvas. Indeed, this composition was rejected for the final painting, in which figures and boats are again placed in the foreground, and the surrounding landscape reduced, although areas of the hills at the left are retained. Rather, the squaring up appears to have been the means by which the artist assessed the placing, direction and weight of compositional elements in this rapid, searching drawing.　　　w.b.

Antoine Watteau (1684–1721)

A Faun c.1712–15

Preliminary drawing with red chalk; black chalk, with some detailed drawing in red chalk, and heightening with white chalk, applied with the moist brush; on buff (discoloured) laid paper. The sheet unevenly trimmed on all sides, to a ruled line in pen and iron gall ink, 28.5 × 21.1
Collector's mark: Baron L.A. de Schwiter, lower left (Lugt, 1768).

Princes Gate Collection

This superb drawing is a study for a lost painting of *Autumn*, one of a series of *The Four Seasons* which was commissioned by the wealthy collector Pierre Crozat for the dining room of his house in the rue de Richelieu some time between 1712 and 1715. Of the four oval paintings only *Summer* now survives and is in the National Gallery of Washington (Samuel H. Kress Coll.): the absence of *Spring*, *Autumn*, and *Winter* is barely compensated by small indifferent engravings, which have nevertheless enabled the series to be comprehended as a suite. The beauty, size, and importance of the large blonde figure of *Summer* indicates the sumptuousness of the commission and the unusual inventiveness which Watteau brought to its execution. It was a commission which removed him from his habitual preoccupation with the theatre and obliged him to work within the wider tradition of European allegorical painting.

The Princes Gate drawing is an extremely strong and forthright visualisation of a satyr: he holds a wine bottle in either hand and his features are slanted and goatlike. The engraving after the finished composition shows him half-length, pouring wine for a Bacchus at whose feet a reclining half-dressed nymph proffers a glass. Both the satyr and the nymph were suggested by Titian's large mythology, *The Bacchanal of the Andrians*, in the Prado, Madrid. It is thought that the link between the Titian original and Watteau's derivation may have been provided by the painter La Fosse who is said to have furnished sketches from which Watteau worked. Legend also has it that Crozat returned from Italy in 1715 with a harvest of Italian drawings which presumably included a direct source, or if not a direct source, drawings of sufficient mastery to stimulate Watteau into producing some of his finest studies, of which this is assuredly one.

Both legends lack the evidence to make them secure. The Princes Gate drawing would seem to deny all reliance on secondary sources, and is, although close in spirit to the Titian, exceptionally free in its characterisation. The powerful arms, slanted features, and hairy body, executed in broad and confident strokes of the chalk, have a pagan exuberance even more overt than Titian's calm and stolid wine-pourer, although the expression of Watteau's figure is characteristically withdrawn.

Associated with this drawing is a study of a naked man with two wine bottles in the W.C. Baker Coll., New York. The Baker drawing, however, is clearly made from a nude model: his face wears the patient uninvolved expression of someone merely doing a job of work. The Princes Gate drawing, on the other hand, is alive with the true spirit of paganism. A.B.

Giovanni Antonio Canal, called Canaletto (1697–1768)

A View from Somerset Gardens, looking toward London Bridge c.1750

Traces of preliminary drawing in graphite both free-hand and ruled; contour drawing in pen and iron gall ink; brush and carbon black ink washes, with some drawing with the point and the flat of the brush; on pale buff (stained) laid paper. The sheet edged with a double ruled line in graphite and carbon black ink wash, unevenly trimmed on all sides. The sheet extensively discoloured and abraded, left, and a rectangle 7.1×6.7 cut from and replaced at the centre left-side. Traces of a vertical fold centre and tears repaired upper left and centre. *Maxima*: 23.5×73.2

Princes Gate Collection

Canaletto left Venice for England in 1746 and stayed there for a decade. From the start of his career in the early 1720s he had attracted English patrons, and from about 1730 the merchant, Joseph Smith, who from 1744 was English Consul in Venice, put a great deal of work in his way. The reduction in English tourists to Venice after the outbreak of the War of the Austrian Succession in 1741 is usually seen as the main reason why the artist took the drastic step of pursuing his patrons back to their own country, though he is known to have been encouraged to go by the decorative painter Amigoni, one of the long list of Italian painters, architects and stuccadors who had successfully sought work in England earlier in the century.

Canaletto's pellucid vision of London may misrepresent the atmosphere, but it provides a vivid idea of the dominance of classical architecture there by the mid-century. This view is one of a pair taken from the river terrace of Somerset House, one looking west, and this one looking east towards the city, over which rise the massive bulk and dome of S. Paul's Cathedral and the wonderful array of Wren's church steeples. Away to the right the Monument can be seen and the arches of Old London Bridge. In the foreground is the white Portland stone of Inigo Jones's river stairs of 1628–32.

Five autograph versions are known of this composition, three paintings and two drawings. This is the larger and finer of the drawings and on it Canaletto seems to have based the recently rediscovered painting now in the Paul Mellon Collection, which was recorded in an engraving by E. Rooker dated 1750.   J.A.N.

detail

Giovanni Antonio Canal, called Canaletto (1697–1768)

The Piazza di S. Giacomo di Rialto c.1760

Traces of preliminary drawing in graphite, both free-hand and ruled;
contour drawing in pen and golden-brown ink (probably bistre and iron
gall mixture); brush and restricted golden-brown ink washes, and brush
and carbon black ink washes; on white (stained) laid paper.
Strips of paper 1.4 × 41.2 and 1.7 × 2 glued to lower left and right of sheet.
Pictorial area enclosed by artist's ruled line in pen and golden brown ink.
Maxima: 31.85 × 43.3
Signed in pen and iron gall ink, on a strip of joined paper below the
pictorial area, lower left 'Antonio Canal del:' and inscribed by the artist in
pen and iron gall ink 'Piazza di S. Giaccomo di Rialto in Venezia, con
parte del Famoso Ponte in distanza, Versso S. Bartolm:^{co}' at the centre of
the strip of paper.
Collector's mark: Marquis de Lagoy, lower right (Lugt, 1710)

Princes Gate Collection

No one has ever produced more delectable holiday souvenirs than
Canaletto. The little piazza in front of the church of S. Giacomo di Rialto is
still today on a main tourist route through Venice; one can dive into the
shops in the Ruga degli Orefici, where goldsmiths used to trade, before being
swept with the crowd up and over the Rialto Bridge beyond.

So, in spite of the architectural modesty of the scene, Canaletto seems to have
established it at an early date among his standard views of the city. A
painting of it in Dresden must date from shortly before 1730, and another, in
Ottawa, probably belongs to the mid-1740s. This drawing however is a late
work, datable stylistically c.1760. The artist did not however visit the scene
afresh, but had recourse to earlier sketches, for the spire of the church of
S. Bartolomeo visible over the rooftops to the right was dismantled in 1747
and rebuilt in its present bulbous form quite different from what Canaletto
shows here. What is more, the columns of the loggia fronting the church,
correctly shown as five in the earlier painting, reduced to four in the later
painting, are here increased to six!

Nevertheless, this drawing is an outstandingly fine example of Canaletto's
draughtsmanship. It has been suggested that the artist's careful signature
and identification of the scene may have been added because the drawing
was to be engraved. This would have made the view much more widely
available to tourists, although, in fact, no engraving of this view is known.

J.A.N.

Piazza di S. Giaccomo di Rialto in Venezia, con parte del Famoso Ponte in distanza, Versso S. Bartolm.eo

Giovanni Battista Tiepolo (1696–1770)

The Holy Family late 1750s

Preliminary drawing in black chalk; pen and bistre; brush and grey-brown ink wash, with some drawing with the point and flat of the brush; on thin white laid paper. The sheet unevenly trimmed on all sides.
Maxima: 28 × 20

Samuel Courtauld Collection

This drawing, along with three others in the Princes Gate Collection, belonged to a group of nearly 70 studies of the Holy Family made by Tiepolo in the late 1750s. They, and numerous head studies, were preserved in one of nine albums of drawings put together in Giambattista's lifetime and deposited in the monastery library of the Somaschi Fathers at S. Maria della Salute just before the departure of Giambattista, Domenico, and Lorenzo for Madrid in 1762. It may be mentioned that Tiepolo's second surviving son, Giuseppe Maria, was a priest at the Salute.

Following the suppression of the monastery in 1810, the albums passed through various hands and were sold by Sotheby's in 1885 before a more general dispersal. The album containing the Holy Family studies was finally broken up for sale in 1928 by the Savile Gallery, London, who held an exhibition of 40 items in which our drawing was number four. The series is a remarkable set of variations on a theme which George Knox thinks may have occupied Giambattista at a time when gout restricted his normal activities. The central Holy Family is frequently accompanied by other figures: the little S. John the Baptist, S. Anne, and a variety of angels. S. Joseph himself fills a number of rôles: the affectionate father, an adoring saint, a curious onlooker, and even a reader seeking enlightenment or re-assurance. To some of the groups there is a background of hinted architectural elements, and to some a traditional Venetian tree.

The Courtauld study, however, is of the three central figures. The lines and touches of black chalk, left faint and unfulfilled, may indicate that Tiepolo changed his mind as he proceeded. What might have been a portrayal of the Family now almost suggests a sort of triune Assumption or Apotheosis – there is no terrestial background and no earthly stability below – and has become a heavenly conversation piece. A dramatic unity it certainly is, effectively defined by the generous use of wash. Joseph seems puzzled, even troubled; the Virgin is thoughtful, perhaps recalling Gabriel's words at the Annunciation; the Christ Child looks ahead, as it were, with innocent confidence. No related painting is known for this drawing or for any of the others in the series. Each is complete in itself and, as James Byam Shaw has commented: 'They are all masterpieces in which the draughtsman is working out a motif or practising his invention and sleight of hand.'   R.H.

Giovanni Battista Tiepolo (1696–1770)

An Angel holding a Monstrance c.1769–70

Red chalk, heightened with white chalk; on grey-blue (stained) laid paper (watermarked 'WM'). The sheet trimmed on all sides to an uneven shape.
Maxima: 31.6 × 25.3
Inscribed in an old hand in iron gall ink, *verso*: '48.[the '4' altered from '3'] X^{rs} N° 3190' (artist's price and number? 'Xrs' is a Spanish abbreviation for 'reales').

Princes Gate Collection

Giambattista Tiepolo, with sons and assistants, went to Madrid in 1762, in response to an invitation from Charles III of Spain to decorate the Royal Palace. The decoration was completed in 1766, and in the following year Tiepolo was commissioned to paint seven altarpieces (including that for the high altar) for S. Pascual Baylon, the monastery church of the Discalced Franciscans at Aranjuez, south of Madrid. Our drawing is clearly a late preparatory thought for the high altarpiece, the *modello* for which (along with those for four of the other altarpieces) is in the Princes Gate Collection.

The finished altarpiece, portraying S. Pascual's Vision of the Eucharist, is now known only through two fragments in the Prado and Domenico Tiepolo's etching of the whole work. The etching and one of the fragments reveal a difference from the *modello*: the angel holding the monstrance is no longer wearing the humeral veil which is worn over the hands of the celebrant at processions of the Blessed Sacrament and at Benediction. The change must have been made after the formal approval of the *modelli* in September 1767, and possibly not until after the final submission of the altarpieces in August 1769, when Tiepolo expressed his willingness to amend anything that was not royally approved.

It has been thought that the king or his confessor, Padre Joaquin de Eleta, may have raised some objection to the wearing of the veil by an angel, to meet which objection Tiepolo would have executed our drawing, preparatory to incorporating the amendment in the altarpiece itself. But it is noteworthy that, with the disappearance of the priestly veil, an equally priestly stole has been introduced (worn crossed as formerly at Mass or Benediction), and it is thus possible that the amendment, rather than reflecting a theological nicety, was made for pictorial reasons by Tiepolo himself, perhaps while the paintings were still in his studio during the winter of 1769/1770.

Whatever the circumstances of the change, however, we must be thankful for this beautiful drawing. Made during the last years, perhaps even the last months, of his life, it shows no diminution of energy or imagination. In fact the vigour with which it has been executed, the sureness of touch with which the white heightening has been applied, and the delicacy of drawing of the angel's costume, all suggest a creative excitement which one associates with a younger artist, but by which an older man – Tiepolo was approaching his middle seventies – may only occasionally be visited. We are fortunate to be able to enjoy the fruit of such a visitation.   R.H.

Jean-Honoré Fragonard (1732–1806)

La Résignée 1765

Red chalk; on off-white laid paper. The sheet edged with a ruled line in pen and carbon black ink, and laid down on an 18th (?)-century mount, 22.5 × 17.2
Signed and dated in pen and iron gall ink, lower left: 'frago.1765'
Collectors' marks: de Goncourt brothers, lower right (Lugt, 1089); blind stamp on mount, below the sheet, left, anonymous collector (Lugt, 2890).

Princes Gate Collection

The subject of this drawing has not been identified. The names of Marie-Anne Gérard, Fragonard's wife, Rosalie, his daughter, and Marguerite Gérard, his sister-in-law, have all been suggested but can be discounted. Fragonard married in 1770, his daughter was born a year earlier, and his sister-in-law did not arrive in Paris until 1775. The Princes Gate drawing is signed and dated 1765, although the date has been persistently misread as 1785 owing to its close resemblance to a drawing of a seated girl wearing an identical dress and with arms in the same position in the former collection of Florence J. Gould, sold Sotheby Parke Bernet, New York, April 1985.

The distance between the two dates – 1765 and 1785 – is puzzling, as is the fact that the models look very like each other. But the dates can be clearly read and there are divergencies: the girl in the Gould drawing wears a cap and a ribbon round her neck, while the woman in the Princes Gate drawing is perceptibly older. The costume would appear to be some kind of *déshabillé*, perhaps belonging to the Fragonard household or studio and used as a prop. In any event both drawings are clearly done from the model. Both show Fragonard in an unusual mood of naturalism, slowing down his normal vivacity to produce quieter more reflective observations: the Princes Gate drawing in particular shows some influence from Fragonard's contemporary, Greuze, who pioneered the taste for homeliness in genre painting, not without salacious undertones, and was himself an outstanding draughts-man. The shading of the ground in the Princes Gate drawing is particularly close to Greuze.

In 1765, the date of the Princes Gate drawing, Fragonard was both famous and notorious. This year marked his presentation to the Academy of his formal reception work, *Corresus and Callirhoe* (Louvre) which caused a sensation when it was shown in the Salon. A huge and excited painting, it seemed to mark out Fragonard for future commissions, which he nevertheless declined. There is evidence that he was of a domestic turn of mind, or that intimism beguiled him. Certainly the Princes Gate drawing is an independent study, and not a study for a painting. The title, *La Résignée*, which first appears in the catalogue of an exhibition of French 18th-century art in Berlin in 1910, is fanciful: the face of the girl exhibits nothing more than the languour of someone told to sit still and hold the pose.

Fragonard was an accomplished performer in red chalk, a technique which he inherited from Watteau, but his preference for the medium here, as opposed to his more customary black chalk, bistre or sepia, as well as the unusual stolidity of the drawing, argues an adherence to the quieter virtues of *sensibilité*, a mode still in favour in the 1760s. Discarding his habitual moods of fervour and imaginative energy, Fragonard here discloses the quieter side of his nature. His generally peaceable disposition was to stand him in good stead during the Revolution, which he survived, thanks largely to the protection of David on whom he was an outstanding influence. A.B.

Paul Sandby (1730/1–1809)

The Henry VIII Gateway, Windsor 1767

Graphite, watercolour and bodycolour on white wove paper, 37 × 47.1
on artist's mount, 39.5 × 49.9
Signed, lower left: 'P Sandby Pinx^t 1767'

Spooner Collection

Paul Sandby takes his place alongside Gainsborough and Richard Wilson as a founder of the British landscape school, even though he worked not in oil but in bodycolour and the topographical element is much stronger in his work than in theirs.

The scenes from which he principally drew inspiration were Windsor Castle, Park and Forest. His elder brother, Thomas, the draughtsman and architect, had from 1746 been on the staff of William Augustus, Duke of Cumberland, who held the post of Ranger of Windsor Forest. During the 1750s and 1760s Paul recorded the Castle and its environs from every conceivable angle, frequently peopling his scenes with wittily-observed local characters.

In this drawing Sandby gives a remarkable close-up view of the archway of the Great or Town Gate of the Castle, with a glimpse through it of the timber-framed houses of the town. The Gate, at the south-west angle of the outer ward, had been constructed by Henry VIII *c.*1510–16. One of its functions from the beginning had been as the 'Exchequer, wherein the Court and Records of the Honour' were kept, so it perhaps naturally evolved into a prison. The debtors' prison was not removed from the Gate until shortly after 1790.

Sandby has had his fun with this. On the south turret is fixed a notice: 'Please Remember the Poor Confin'd Debtors', one of whom, peering from a grille high above, has poked out a rod to dangle down a rope with a purse on the end. Into this a perhaps drunken man seems to be trying to drop a coin, while a servant woman restrains him. From one side lounging soldiers look on, and a pot-bellied carter from the other. On the left a half-torn notice advertises 'WINDSOR and EATON MACH. Sold out'.

The artists' organisations which were successively founded in London in the mid-18th century were strongly supported by the Sandby brothers. Paul exhibited at the Society of Artists from 1763 to 1768, before becoming, with his brother, a founder member of the Royal Academy.

This exceptionally highly finished drawing, signed by the artist in gold, was probably one of his last two exhibits at the Society of Artists, in 1768. A monochrome sketch of this subject, and a water-colour in which the figure groups are less elaborately disposed, are in the Royal Collection.   J.A.N.

Thomas Gainsborough (1727–88)

A Road through a Wood, with Figures on Horseback and on Foot mid-1780s

Black chalk; brown and grey ink, with drawing with point of the brush; heightening with white oil paint; yellow varnish; on pale buff laid paper, 22.1 × 30.5
Numbered by the artist(?) in graphite, *verso*: '1'.
The composition, with variations, was engraved in aquatint and published by J. & J. Boydell in 1797 as no.12 of a series of 12.

Witt Collection

Gainsborough began experimenting with drawings using mixed media such as chalk, ink, wash, oil and varnish in the early 1770s. This drawing, however, dates from the mid-1780s and such later works with mixed media can be identified by the thicker and more impasted use of white lead for highlights compared with the more broken application of white in the earlier drawings. In a letter of 29 January 1773 Gainsborough had revealed to his friend William Jackson his formula telling him 'never to impart my secret to any one living . . .:- make the black and white of your drawing, the Effect I mean, & disposition in rough, Indian ink shaddows & your lights of Bristol made white lead which you buy in lumps at any house painters . . . when you see your effect, dip it all over in skim'd milk . . .'. After describing further processes Gainsborough writes that it should finally be treated as follows, 'float it all over with Gum Water . . . varnish it 3 times with Spirit Varnish such as I sent you.'

It seems Gainsborough wanted in drawings of this kind to achieve some of the body and weight of oil paintings whilst at the same time using a loose, sketchy and undetailed style which would have been considered inappropriate in finished paintings. He exhibited 10 drawings in imitation of paintings at the Royal Academy in 1772. Drawings, especially landscape drawings, were an important part of Gainsborough's output and they were greatly admired in his own lifetime, William Jackson writing 'No man ever possessed methods so various in producing effect, and all excellent . . .'.

Like the great majority of Gainsborough's landscapes the subject is taken from imagination and remembrances of countryside and also paintings, especially Dutch and Flemish 17th-century painters such as Rubens and Wynants, rather than from a particular location. Many of his landscapes were drawn or painted in the evening by candlelight after his day had been spent in the business of portrait painting. He used bits of coal, broccoli, glass and other small objects to make an arrangement which he could use as a basis from which to create a landscape. As in this drawing, his landscape compositions are usually generalised and often have the lumpy, humpy character dictated by a compositional beginning as a tabletop arrangement of odd bits of vegetation and stones. Gainsborough's intention, from such mundane origins, seems to have been to create in the spectator a mood of 'quietness and ease', as he said himself, and his gentle pastorals are unspecific and non-literary. The peasant figures re-inforce this mood of ease and introduce into the landscape a sense of human involvement with and response to its beauties.   J.S.

Alexander Cozens (1717–86)

A Blasted Tree in a Landscape c.1780

Traces of preliminary drawing in graphite; washes in brown ink, with drawing with pen and the point of the brush; slight additions of gum or varnish in the foreground darks; on very thin laid paper, prepared with a ground of dilute varnish. The drawing edged with vestiges of a ruled line in pen and black ink, and laid down on the artist's mount, unevenly trimmed, 31.5 × 40.5 on mount, 32.2 × 41.3
Signed in pen and grey ink on the mount, lower left: 'Alex.ʳ Cozens.'.
Collector's mark, blind stamp lower left, 'B·W' (Benjamin West P.R.A.: Lugt, 419) above artist's signature.

Spooner Collection

This is, for Alexander Cozens, a highly finished and quite large composition. It was done in monochrome which is typical in his drawings. Alexander's landscape drawings are almost always invented and generalized. They do not depict particular places, but they follow his interest in the classification of natural phenomena in a systematic way. They are also conditioned by his concern with the actual process of creating a composition.

Both these concerns, that of classification and that of process, show him as a teacher as indeed he was, working at Christ's Hospital and later Eton College. He also produced a number of didactic books on landscape and art. William Beckford, his friend and patron, called him, in 1781, about the time he made this drawing, '. . . almost as full of Systems as the Universe.'

At the very end of his life appeared his *A New Method of Assisting the Invention in Drawing Original Compositions of Landscape*. This put forward his long-established and long-taught practice of using random 'blots' of ink wash as the basis for creating a landscape composition. In this drawing it is almost certain that the composition was traced through from a 'blot' which would have dictated the overall lines of the composition, the thin paper having been made semi-transparent by the thin ground of varnish. The idea of using a random blot was partly derived from Leonardo da Vinci's well-known remarks about being able to see compositions in old walls.

Most of Alexander's landscapes based on 'blots' may be 'invented', but they also follow in many cases quite closely the compositional principles and effects of classical landscape as expressed in the works of Claude, Poussin, and Salvator Rosa. They did, however, encourage the artist or pupil to see in terms of mass and tone rather than in terms of outline.

Alexander Cozens was also interested in classifying natural phenomena such as skies and trees. His depictions of skies appeared in *A New Method* . . . and were meant to accompany the 'blot' landscapes. His interest in trees is shown by his 1771 publication *The Shape, Skeleton and Foliage of Thirty-two Species of Trees*. In this drawing the blasted oak seems to suggest a knowledge of Salvator Rosa's art as much as any model in reality.

J.S.

John Robert Cozens (1752–97)

The Castel Sant'Angelo, Rome 1780

Graphite; black ink, and blue watercolour washes; some slight scraping out; on white (now unevenly discoloured) laid paper. The sheet unevenly trimmed on all sides, and laid down on the artist's mount, also unevenly trimmed, 36 × 52.6 on mount 41.5 × 58
The sheet watermarked with a shield bearing the design of a fleur-de-lis, surmounted by a crown. The mount watermarked 'J WHATMAN'.
Signed in pen and black ink, bottom left of centre: 'Jn.º Cozens 1780'.
Inscribed in a later hand in pencil, on the back of the mount: 'Castel of St Angelo *Rome*/J.R. Cozens 1780'.

Spooner Collection

This watercolour was executed in England in 1780 and is one of the finished works which John Robert Cozens produced after and as a result of his first journey to Switzerland and Italy (1776–9). This tour was taken in the company of Richard Payne Knight, the connoisseur, writer and collector.

Although there are no other known drawings or watercolours of this composition by Cozens there must almost certainly have been some preliminary study or studies because there are traces of graphite squaring up lines under the area of the castle, strongly suggesting that the composition was transferred by the artist from an earlier work. There is an etching of almost the same view, now thought to have been done in 1746 in Rome by John Robert's father, Alexander Cozens, though previously attributed to the son. This is in reverse of the watercolour, which is in the correct sense of direction, and there is a possibility that the etching may have been done on the spot out of doors, a most unusual practice. If the attribution of the etching to Alexander is correct it would provide an interesting, though quite rare, example of John Robert using one of his father's works as a direct source of inspiration. The Castle and Bridge are extremely similar in the etching and the watercolour, both including the smoke from the castle and just the first two arches of the bridge, but John Robert has added the foreground framing device of building, river bank and tiny fishermen as well as the boat. The resulting composition is grander, with the castle appearing more clearly defined and yet more distanced from the spectator.

In contrast to the almost abstract theorising of his father about landscape, John Robert's paintings are always of actual places, depicted with a highly developed subtlety of tone and delicacy of brushwork which matches and helps to instil into the spectator a mood of emotional response. The subject matter of his watercolours of Switzerland and Italy was in line with contemporary taste, comprising both the 'Sublime' grandeur of the Alps and the attraction of Italy with its classical past and landscape associated with the great 17th-century landscape painters such as Claude and Poussin. The Castel Sant'Angelo on the Tiber was a frequently painted landmark which expressed the massive yet marred grandeur of classical Rome.

John Robert's ability to capture atmosphere, both meteorological and emotional, is unique in the watercolour painting of his time and he was greatly admired by later landscape painters such as Turner and Constable. His colour is remarkably restricted, even more so than that of his contemporaries, and this limitation of colour largely to greys and blues, as in this drawing, cannot be fully explained, even given the tendency of watercolourists of the time to have a limited palette dominated by underlying grey wash. It may owe a great deal to the almost entirely monochrome work of his father.   J.S.

John Robert Cozens (1752–97)

London from Greenwich Hill c.1791–3

Graphite; black and brown ink, and restricted watercolour washes; with some drawing with the point of the brush, and the use of the dry brush; redrawing of foreground detail with pen and point of the brush in blue-grey wash, and black and brown ink; on off-white (now unevenly discoloured) wove paper. The sheet unevenly trimmed on all sides, to a ruled line in graphite, 36.9 × 53.5
Signed in pen and black ink, lower left of centre: 'Jnọ Cozens'.

Spooner Collection

The view of London and the River Thames from the heights above Greenwich had been popular with artists for over a hundred years before Cozens took it as his subject. Since the early years of the 18th century Wren domes had dominated the scene, the twin domes of Greenwich Royal Hospital (Royal Naval College) in the foreground, and in the distance S. Paul's Cathedral. Cozens has chosen as his viewpoint One Tree Hill, in the south-east corner of Greenwich Park, from where Limehouse Reach appears in the middle distance, with scores of high-masted ships moored along the Deptford shore.

John Robert Cozens had developed his highly personal, imaginative vision of the grandeur of landscape during two visits to Italy, first in 1776–9, when he travelled in the company of the art theorist and critic Richard Payne Knight, and then in 1782–3 with William Beckford, the novelist and gothic enthusiast. Studies made during these Italian years provided the exclusive subject matter of his watercolours until the last two or three years of his career.

During the early 1790s Cozens finally began to tackle English subjects. This drawing shows his typically restricted range of grey, blue, green and brown washes, yet it depicts a completely un-Italian scene undistorted by memories of Italy. Cozens' response to the groves of oak and chestnut tumbling across the hillside and the hazy city beyond is fresh and true.

Six autograph versions of this design are known. One is dated 1791, and they must all belong to the period shortly before 1793, when Cozens became so incapacitated by illness that he could no longer practice his art.   J.A.N.

Francis Towne (c.1740–1816)

In the Valley of the Grisons 1781

Traces of preliminary drawing in graphite; drawing with pen and brown-grey ink in foreground; yellow, green, brown and blue watercolour washes and grey ink wash, with some drawing with the point of the brush; additions of gum or varnish to enhance the darks of foreground shadows; on white laid paper. The sheet laid down on the artist's mount.

The mount, a design of five ruled bands in graphite; alternate bands in dark and pale grey wash; on pale buff laid paper. The mount unevenly trimmed on all sides, the bottom right corner cut.

The main sheet watermarked with a shield with fleur-de-lis design, surmounted by a coronet, 28.7 × 46.7; on mount 38.8 × 57.2 Signed in pen and black ink, lower left of centre: 'F. Towne delt/N.19 1781', and inscribed by the artist in pen and brown ink on the back of the mount: 'N°19/In the Valley of the Grisons looking on (?) [apparently altered by the artist from 'to'] Tusis . . . in the morning drawn by Francis Towne on the spot.' (the 'n' of 'on' and 'Tusis' strengthened by a later hand in black ink; after 'Tusis' an area of erasure, although the tail of a 'g' or 'y' is still visible).

Spooner Collection

Francis Towne's work, of which this is a fine example, always has a strong architectural character, and he delineates his subject-matter with precision and grand simplicity.

From the artist's own description of the site of this drawing, it would seem to show a view looking south and upstream along River Viamala to Thusis (the 'Tusis' of the artist's inscription) in the Graubünden (the German name by which the Canton of Grisons is now known). The high peaks in the distance are probably Curver, Grisch and Platta. The town of Reichenau, on the Upper Rhine of which the Viamala is a tributary, would lie behind the artist as he sketched this scene from a vantage point above the road on the west bank of the river. Towne visited Italy in 1780, returning through Switzerland in 1781, and this highly finished sheet would seem to have been executed on the spot, rather than worked up in the studio from preliminary sketches.

The sheet size of this drawing does not appear to correspond in any way to those which came from Towne's own collection, and described by A.P. Oppé as used by him for his Italian and Swiss drawings. He also describes them as, 'practically all are fully dated'. Nor do the numbers correspond to those recorded by Oppé, although he refers to one series, on thin laid paper, $8\frac{1}{4} \times 6\frac{1}{8}$ ins. (21 × 15.5 cm.), with a numerical sequence 16 to 59.

Oppé refers to the 'severity' of Towne's Swiss views. There is no sentiment or 'prettiness', and the mountains are seen as 'hard and cruel and too imminent and hostile to permit any thought of rustic bliss or primitive innocence in the valleys at their base. He is overpowered, almost obsessed, by the mountains themselves.'

D.F.

Thomas Girtin (1775–1802)

Peterborough Cathedral from the West Front c.1794

Graphite and watercolour; preliminary drawing in soft graphite, both free-hand, and, in the foreground, ruled; red, brown, blue and grey watercolour washes, with drawing with the point of the brush; possibly a very dilute blue bodycolour in the sky; extensive drawing of architectural details with pen and the point of the brush in black, grey and brown ink washes; on white wove paper (the drawing faded except at the edges where protected by an earlier mount), 40.7 × 27.1

Spooner Collection

'If Tom Girtin had lived I should have starved.' Thus J.M.W. Turner about an artist who was his exact contemporary and whom he greatly admired. Turner's meaning is a lttle ambiguous, for although Girtin quickly established a following for his work among certain collectors who bought his work at quite high prices, he did not enjoy the meteoric rise in the ranks of the Royal Academy that distinguished Turner's career, who became a full Academician at the age of 27 in 1802 – the same year in which Girtin died.

Girtin accompanied the artist, James Moore, on a tour of the Midlands in 1794, when he visited Lincoln, Lichfield, Stratford-upon-Avon, and Warwick, as well as Peterborough. His drawings of Peterborough Cathedral show a remarkable mastery of perspective and an unusual maturity for an artist of only nineteen. This composition, one of six known variations on the theme, is among his boldest and most imaginative conceptions. The Spooner sheet seems to be the first of the watercolours based on the pencil study now in the Mellon Collection. Two watercolours of the same subject are signed and dated 1794 (one of these is in the Ashmolean Museum, Oxford). Our watercolour appears to pre-date the version in the Whitworth Art Gallery, Manchester; for in the Spooner sheet, the artist has drawn a horizontal ruled line in graphite at 2.5cm. from the bottom of the watercolour, which probably indicates his intention to crop the composition at this point. An intention that is carried out in the Whitworth composition, which finishes at exactly the same point, and the Cathedral spire has also been completely eliminated from this version, presumably to avoid a top-heavy composition. These refinements support the idea that the Spooner watercolour, which shows the whole of the West Front as viewed from a more distant vantage point, is earlier than the Whitworth sheet, where a more dramatic close-up view is depicted. D.F.

190

John Sell Cotman (1782–1842)

Doorway to the Refectory, Kirkham Abbey, Yorkshire 1804

Pencil and watercolour; detailed preliminary drawing in soft pencil; restricted colour washes, with some drawing with the point of the brush; touches of dilute white and pale green body colour; some slight additions of gum or varnish in the darks of the foreground foliage; on off-white wove paper. The sheet laid down (? by the artist) on buff wove paper, 37.8 × 26.6
Signed in pen and brown ink, lower right: 'J.S. Cotman/1804–'.
Inscribed by the artist in pencil on the backing paper: 'Kirkham Abbey/ Yorkshire'. Inscribed in pencil in different hands on backing paper: 'Cotman', 'H.G. Green', and 'Colnaghi'.

Spooner Collection

John Sell Cotman was born in Norwich and came to London in 1798, where he first coloured aquatints for the printseller, Ackermann. He was then employed by Dr. Thomas Munro (who had also employed Girtin and Turner) in making watercolours for drawing-copies. Cotman returned to Norwich in 1806 and became a prominent member of the Norwich Society of Artists. In 1834 he was appointed Drawing Master to King's College, London.

His subtle range of colour and tone, particularly as here, in his architectural work, capture the solidity of the forms with breathtaking beauty. The sombre colours of the masonry act as a perfect foil to the dramatic vista of blue sky and distant landscape which we glimpse through the refectory doorway. Cotman first visited Kirkham Abbey with Paul Sandby Munn in July 1803, and made 'some exquisite drawings of it' according to their hostess, Mrs Cholmeley of Brandsby Hall. She and Cotman spent the day there on 30 August. Cotman made a second tour of Yorkshire in 1804, and a final one in July 1805. This watercolour was presumably based on a drawing made on his first visit. He etched it for his *Miscellaneous Etchings*, 1811.   D.F.

John Constable (1776–1837)

East Bergholt Church c.1817

Hard and soft pencil, with use of the ruler; on off-white (now unevenly discoloured) wove paper. The sheet unevenly trimmed on all sides, to a ruled line in pencil, 31.7 × 23.8

Spooner Collection

This carefully meditated and heavily worked pencil drawing, almost like a soft-ground etching, is not what we usually associate with the name of Constable. It belongs to a small group of finished pencil drawings made in the years around 1815–17, some of which, though probably not this one, were exhibited at the Royal Academy.

This and two other drawings of East Bergholt church, one exhibited in 1818, must date from the long holiday which Constable took with his wife at his family home in the late summer and early autumn of 1817. His father's death the previous year, followed by his marriage to Maria Bicknell, a marriage so long opposed by her grandfather, Dr Rhudde, the rector of East Bergholt, must have given this visit special significance for the artist. During these weeks he made no less than six views of the church porch and tower, pencil and oil sketches as well as the group of three finished drawings of which this is one.

East Bergholt church is famous for its 16th-century timber-framed belfry standing in one corner of the churchyard. But this must have been an expedient when the mighty west tower, begun in 1525, was abandoned well below the bell stage. Had it been completed the tower would have rivalled those nearby towers which Constable knew so well, at Dedham and Stoke-by-Nayland. There was indeed barely space for it in the churchyard; the arch visible on the right of the drawing was for the processional route which had to encircle the church within the churchyard, and was thus forced to pass under the tower. Constable dramatically emphasised the tower's cramped position, making the light fall brightly on the base of the turret which pushes through the churchyard wall. He also indicates the rough patches where areas of flintwork have fallen off. Should one see deliberate intent in Constable's choice and treatment of this subject, this study of frustration and decay?   J.A.N.

Joseph Mallord William Turner (1775–1851)

The Crook of Lune, looking towards Hornby Castle c.1816–18

Traces of preliminary drawing in pencil; watercolour, with use of the dry brush and drawing with the point of the brush; touches of white and other coloured bodycolour, especially in the foliage, bridge, figures and animals; extensive scraping out in the whites (especially in the river), some retinting and some rubbing, also scoring with the point of the brush handle (in vegetation and trees on left of middle-ground); traces of gum or thin varnish in the foreground; some black chalk (in rocks, centre foreground); slight use of finger-printing in grey and brown watercolour; on white wove paper, now backed. Two tears repaired; paper made up in sky, 29.1 × 42.9

Sir Stephen Courtauld Collection

Some of Turner's early success, and certainly the foundation of his fortune, was owed to the volumes of engravings after his topographical views, the first of which appeared in 1814: *Picturesque Views on the Southern Coast of England*.

This is one of Turner's watercolours for 20 views engraved after his designs for *The History of Richmondshire*, published by Longman's between 1819 and 1823. He received the commission from the antiquarian and topographer, Dr. Thomas Dunham Whitaker, early in 1816, and executed the finished watercolours between 1816 and 1818 at a fee of 25 guineas each. It was a high-quality publication, and the engravers were paid between 60 and 80 guineas per plate. However, the original intention of producing a much larger series covering the whole of Yorkshire was abandoned because of the cost, although the publication in its final form was regarded a success. The 20 plates, with a new commentary, were last reprinted as late at 1891.

The series deals with that part of the North Riding bordering on Westmorland and Lancashire, of which the town of Richmond is the centre, and includes some of the finest dales and valleys of the region. It was also a part of the country that J.S. Cotman had painted. The present sheet shows a wide panoramic view of the River Lune, with a glimpse of Hornby Castle in the distance. The high viewpoint, technical complexity and virtuosity of this watercolour is characteristic of the whole series. The range of delicate hues of green-blues, golds and browns suggest a landscape seen through a heat haze suffused by brilliant sunlight.

Ruskin much admired this group of watercolours, and praised them for their warmth of feeling, sense of mass and fidelity to the minutiae of nature. He tried to persuade, unsuccessfully, the University of Oxford to purchase this sheet and *Kirby Lonsdale* (from the same series) in 1884, at the time of his resignation from the Slade Professorship, when they were put on the market by C. Orme, a member of Longman's the publishers. D.F.

Joseph Mallord William Turner (1775–1851)

Colchester c.1825–26

Traces of preliminary drawing in pencil; watercolour, with drawing with the point of the brush and use of the dry brush; white and other coloured bodycolour; touches of white, red, and other coloured chalks; scraping out, and scoring into the wet paint with the point of the brush handle; on white laid paper, the upper half of which, except for the area of the sun, given a very pale grey wash. The sheet laid on pale grey-green paper, 28.8 × 40.7

Sir Stephen Courtauld Collection

This is Turner's finished watercolour for one of the subjects in the largest and most ambitious series of engravings ever produced from his designs, the *Picturesque Views in England and Wales*, which was published in 96 plates between 1827 and 1838. Turner received the commission from Charles Heath (1785–1848), probably in the summer of 1825. He is said to have received from the publishers 60 to 70 guineas for each of the watercolours, but despite their high quality and the technical excellence of the prints, which were executed by a team of engravers under the artist's close supervision, the series was a commercial failure almost from the start, unlike *The History of Richmondshire*, and virtually bankrupted the principal publisher, Heath.

Colchester was one of the first prints to be published in an engraving by Robert Wallis (1794–1878) of 1827. The pencil studies for it (in the 'Norfolk, Suffolk and Essex' sketchbook, Turner Bequest CCIX) were probably done a few years earlier, but Turner only loosely adhered to them, preferring, as was his custom, to treat even quite familiar subjects in a fresh manner, not by falsifying nature but rather enhancing it.

The view shown here is looking south across the River Colne to the town of Colchester, straddled up Middle Hill, with the sunlight streaming through the trees and illuminating the smoky haze above the rooftops of the town. The time of day has been a matter of debate, most commentators have suggested late afternoon, and if so, Turner has either deliberately lowered the sun or lit the scene from imagination.

However, the presence of the sun on the left of the drawing, that is in the south-east, would suggest that the time of day is early morning, in winter. This observation is supported by Ruskin (in his book *Modern Painters*, I, 1843) who, in commenting on the tonal exactitude of Turner's watercolour, asserted that he could '. . . select from among the works named in Chap. V of the next section, pieces of tone absolutely faultless and perfect, from the coolest greys of wintry dawn to the intense fire of summer noon'. In a footnote to this passage, he illustrates Turner's gamut of tone by referring to three watercolours, of which only *Colchester* fits the description of 'wintry dawn'. He later praises Turner's minute and subtle variations of colour and tone by specific reference to this watercolour: 'The drawing of Colchester in the England series, is an example of this delicacy and fullness of tint together with which nothing but nature can be compared.'

The broad sweeping curve of the foreground composition, contrasted with the column of light reflected in the water, anticipate the dramatic effects he was to deploy in his four oils for the dining room at Petworth of the early 1830s. The 'drama' of the hare being chased across the empty foreground, watched by excited spectators, at once animates the scene and unites the two sides of the composition. Turner uses this motive in other works, notably *Apollo and Daphne*, and *Rain, Steam and Speed*.   D.F.

Joseph Mallord William Turner (1775–1851)

Dawn after the Wreck c.1841

Some preliminary drawing in pencil; watercolour, with drawing with the point of the brush; white and other coloured bodycolour; touches of red chalk; rubbing and retinting; on white laid paper.
The drawing edged with a ruled line in pen and brown ink.
The sheet laid on pale green-grey paper, 25.1 × 36.8

Sir Stephen Courtauld Collection

Although this sheet has certain affinities with such oils as *Calais Sands* of 1830, probably done partly in rivalry with, and partly in homage to Richard Parkes Bonington (1802–28), whom Turner had much admired, Ruskin associated it with Turner's 'last years', and a date of about 1841 is generally agreed. The density of paint and the suggestion of colour symbolism both point to the later date, and Dr. John Gage has noted that a similar palette appears in the oil, *The New Moon*, shown at the Royal Academy in 1840 (Tate Gallery, No.526).

Ruskin may perhaps have read more into the work than Turner intended, but the symbolism of death and destruction, of the dog howling in grief at the death of his drowned master, must certainly have been in the artist's mind. Ruskin describes the painting (in *Modern Painters*, V, 1860, part IX, chap.XI): 'The scarlet of the clouds was his symbol of destruction. In his mind it was the colour of blood. So he used it in the Fall of Carthage . . . So he used it in the Slaver [*Slavers throwing overboard the Dead and the Dying – Typhon coming on*, 1840], in the Ulysses [*Ulysses deriding Polyphemus*, 1829], . . .; again in slighter hints and momentary dreams, of which one of the saddest and most tender is a little sketch of dawn, made in his last years. It is a small space of level sea shore; beyond it a fair, soft light in the east; the last storm-clouds melting away, . . .; some little vessel – a collier, probably – has gone down in the night, all hands lost; a single dog has come ashore. Utterly exhausted, its limbs failing under it, and sinking into the sand, it stands howling and shivering. The dawn clouds have the first scarlet upon them, a feeble tinge only, reflected with the same feeble bloodstain on the sand.'   D.F.

Honoré Daumier (1808–79)

The Hypochondriac

Preliminary drawing in black chalk; carbon black ink and restricted watercolour washes, with drawing with both pen and the point of the brush; extensive drawing in black lithographic (?) crayon; on off-white laid paper, 20.7 × 27.1
Signed in pen and carbon black ink wash, lower left: 'h', and below in pen: 'h. Daumier'.

Samuel Courtauld Collection

The possibility of establishing a chronology based on stylistic analysis of Daumier's drawings is remote, since apparently no works on paper were dated by him. The problem is complicated by Daumier's facility as a draughtsman, which was such – as an examination of lithographs executed for newspaper publication, and hence datable, proves – that he was able to draw with equal ease in a variety of manners as the occasion demanded.

The drawing reproduced here relates to a group of works which were inspired by Molière's satire *Le Malade Imaginaire*, among which are two paintings: *The Hypochondriac* (Philadelphia Museum of Art) and *Dr Diafoirus* (Bakwin Coll., New York) which have been dated to 1860–3 and 1870, respectively. It has been suggested that many of the drawings in wash or watercolour treating the subject of doctor and patient may also have been executed during this period, when Daumier's contract with the newspaper *Le Charivari* had been broken.

While thematically related to the Philadelphia painting, in which interest is, however, focused mainly on the figure of Argan (who wears a nightcap tied with a foppish bow similar to that shown here), this drawing is compositionally more closely allied to a charcoal and crayon study of *The Sick Man and Death* (Private Coll., Paris) a drawing whose underlying seriousness places it outside the *Malade Imaginaire* group proper. In this work the patient, whose features, pinched by terror, are a sombre variant of those of Argan seen in the present drawing, lies in profile facing the right, is subject to the contrasting wills of the doctor, right, and Death at the left.

The comic doctors in the Courtauld composition are variants of those who feel the dying man's pulse in the otherwise bitter drawing in Yale University Art Gallery, and are also related to the charlatan who appears in a drawing of *The Hypochondriac* and a preliminary study for it, both of which are now lost. Similar figures of doctors, one of whom is armed with an enormous syringe of the type visible in this drawing, appear in force in a lithograph published in the newspaper *Actualités* of 28 May 1867, captioned 'Yesterday the breech-loading gun, tomorrow those fellows . . .', while perhaps the earliest motif of such a doctor is to be seen, appropriately, in the guise of Aesculapius, in a caricature also published in *Actualités* on 16 March 1859.

W.B.

Edgar Degas (1834–1917)

Seated Woman Adjusting her Hair c.1884?

Chalk and pastel on buff hand-made paper. The drawing made up of two sheets placed edge to edge and laid on white wove paper, 63 × 59.9
Stamped in red, lower right: 'Degas' (Lugt, 658)

Samuel Courtauld Collection

In its present state, this pastel is not a finished work, but it bears a complex relationship to a very similar oil painting. Many changes are visible in the pose of the figure in this pastel, most visibly in the placing of the arms and the line of the left hip, and also in the addition of a wide extra strip of paper across the top of the composition. The oil version corresponds closely to the original state of the pastel before these revisions. Degas more often used pastel in preparatory studies for oils than vice versa, so the present sheet may originally have been a study for the oil; but it was also very probably reworked, and brought into its present form, after the execution of the oil. The relationship between these works, and the final appearance of the present pastel, show how intensively Degas rethought and reformulated his compositional ideas, and how the work of art itself could become a sort of laboratory in which he worked out his ideas, leaving the process very visible when he abandoned the picture.

Seated Woman Adjusting her Hair shows marked difference in execution between its parts; most summary are the notations on the added sheet, and the alterations made to the original composition; the woman's jacket is more fully modelled, and the folds of material at the back of the skirt are unusually crisply treated for Degas' work at this date; the deeply shadowed modelling of these folds is reminiscent of German Renaissance draughtsmanship; Degas had studied Holbein, Cranach and Dürer closely between 1859 and 1864. This elaborate draughtsmanship is set off against the soft reds on the woman's seat and the stronger red verticals of the wall beyond. It seems to have been added late in the execution of the pastel, and thus probably belongs to its reworking, which suggests that Degas was beginning a more complex rethinking of the whole idea, which was left off in this unfinished state.

The subject relates to the theme of the milliners' shops which Degas was exploring in these years. This interest in the world of fashion was part of his wider fascination with the most artifical elements of modern urban life, seen also in his treatment of subjects from the ballet and café-concert.   J.H.

Edgar Degas (1834–1917)

After the Bath, Woman Drying Herself c.1889–90?

Pastel on thin buff wove paper. The drawing made up of two sheets, both laid down on thin buff wove paper, and laid down again on millboard, 67.7 × 57.8

Stamped in red oval, on original backing: 'ATELIER/ED. DEGAS'

Samuel Courtauld Collection

From the mid-1880s onwards, the subject of women bathing in tubs or drying themselves became one of Degas' central preoccupations. At the eighth Impressionist group exhibition in 1886 he exhibited a set of pastels under the collective title *Sequence of Nudes, of Women Bathing, Washing, Drying, Wiping Themselves, Combing their Hair or Having it Combed*; the present pastel probably dates from a few years after this. At around this date he told George Moore that his aims in his pictures of bathing women were to show 'a human creature preoccupied with herself – a cat who licks herself; hitherto, the nude has always been represented in poses which presupposes an audience, but these women of mine are honest and simple folk, unconcerned by any other interests than those involved in their physical condition. . . . It is as if you looked through a key-hole.' Images such as these have at times been seen as misogynist, by critics from J.-K. Huysmans onwards, but they show the same studied detachment of viewpoint as his treatment of many other themes; there is no savagery in the way that his models are presented. The choice of subject, and the way in which he described it to Moore does, though, reiterate the stereotyped male attitude towards the female, as being concerned essentially with the physical world, while the (male) artist looks in on it from outside and above.

By this date Degas was using the pastel medium with great improvisatory freedom, producing a great variety of bold marks – broad swathes of white for the towel, more broken accents and smudges on the background and the chair at lower right, and long thin raking lines on the model's body which cut across its three-dimensional modelling at some points. The figure is treated in soft, pale nuances of pink and green, but surrounded by the strong, hot colour of carpet, wall and chair; blue is sparingly used, only in the bathtub and at points on the carpet.

Despite the informality of the model's pose, the composition is very carefully organised; within a framework of diagonals, of floor and wall, the curving forms of the figure are tucked in between the bath and the chair, and linked to the top left corner by her arm, to the top right by the quickly notated curtain. At a number of points the modelling of the figure is not fully resolved, notably in the treatment of the right arm; moreover, a number of alterations in the position of the figure can be clearly seen particularly along the line of her left arm and her right knee. Presumably the work was abandoned in a provisional state, like virtually all of Degas's later works, when his activities were increasingly hampered by his deteriorating eyesight, which led him to favour the more rapidly malleable medium of pastel, in preference to oil paint.   J.H.

Georges Seurat (1859–91)

Standing Female Nude c.1881–2

Preliminary drawing with stump impregnated with pencil; Conté crayon;
on pale cream (now unevenly discoloured) Michallet paper. All edges of the sheet uneven,
the lower corners torn away, *Maxima*: 63.2 × 48.2
Inscribed by Félix Fénéon in pencil, *verso*: 'de Georges Seurat/fel F' and numbered
in red crayon '381'

Samuel Courtauld Collection

The authorship of this drawing, doubted by certain critics, was upheld by R.L. Herbert in his pioneering study of Seurat's draughtsmanship, published in 1965. The sheet unmistakeably displays Seurat's handling, while the inscription on the *verso* by the artist's friend and champion, the critic Félix Fénéon (who may have owned the drawing), and its inclusion in exhibitions organised by Fénéon in 1920 and 1926 provide additional support for its authenticity.

A line study of the female nude (location unknown) in which the pose of the model shown here is established, was dated by Herbert to 1879, and a similar date was tentatively assigned to the Courtauld drawing. The early dating connects both works to the studies of full-length nudes (the *académies*) drawn from life at the Ecole des Beaux-Arts from c.1875 to 1878, with which there are undeniable affinities.

In this drawing, however, the curving webs of chalk lines over the lighted areas of the torso, the massing of shadows from rectilinear networks of strokes, and the subtle gradations of tone indicating diminishing light over the legs, are characteristics of Seurat's independent draughtsmanship of c.1881–2, the culmination of some three years' logical, rigorous development: and it is to this later date that the drawing should be assigned.

Despite the idealised treatment of the nude here – and comparison with the preliminary sketch reveals that Seurat has repositioned limbs and adjusted contours to create a continuously curving form in which the lines of breast, arms and legs echo each other – the model is nevertheless identifiable as that in the line study. Since this sketch was probably drawn immediately prior to the Courtauld sheet, it should also be redated to c.1881–2.

The Courtauld drawing, in which subject and handling appear to relate to different moments in the artist's career, poses problems of interpretation when placed among other studies of Seurat's early maturity. It seems, however, that the artist returned to the subject of the nude as a touchstone against which the capabilities of his newly established personal draughtsmanship could be tested; and in referring to, rather than reverting to the subject and practices familiar from the Beaux-Arts, Seurat presented a critique of the earlier *académies*. The size of this sheet is approximately that of the Beaux-Arts nudes (which average 63.5 × 48.5 cm., and are larger than those employed early in Seurat's independent career), yet the present subject, the nude female, was rarely treated by the artist during his academic training. The standard academic drawing implement of stump impregnated with graphite, used in the *académies* to create sharply defined shadows of even tone across pallid figures, is here employed at the left of the model to evoke the luminosity of flesh in half light. The graphite becomes a colouristic adjunct to the sensuous modelling of form with Conté crayon, yet the handling, leanness and silvery tone of the medium is compared and contrasted with the personal manner of drawing with the fatty, richly chromatic chalk.

The interpretation of the drawing as both a late extension and critique of the *académies* should not obscure the influence of Seurat's contemporaries upon the work. For it is to the lithographs of Henri Fantin-Latour, an artist at the height of his popularity in the late 1870s, that the buxom form of the model and the manner in which it emerges from shadow are indebted in this unique drawing.   W.B.

Henri de Toulouse-Lautrec (1864–1901)

A Woman lying in Bed 1896

Pencil; touches of brush and carbon black ink or watercolour wash; on off-white laid paper.
The sheet unevenly trimmed, bottom, 30.3 × 48
Signed in pencil, lower left: 'H T-Lautrec' (the initials in monogram)

Samuel Courtauld Collection

The model for this drawing is the prostitute, Pauline Baron, known as Mlle Popo, whose mother owned a brothel at 26 rue des Moulins in Paris, in which Toulouse-Lautrec lived intermittently during 1895 and 1896. The drawing is datable probably to the early months of 1896, since Mlle Popo also appears in four of the suite of 10 lithographs of brothel subjects entitled *Elles*, published in April of that year, as well as in the thematically related print *Le Sommeil*, of the same period.

While the drawing cannot be included among the 12 preparatory designs for motifs or compositions of *Elles*, its subject and handling nevertheless come within the range of certain plates of the series: its mood of quiet, mundane domesticity bordering on tenderness – not normally present in Lautrec's work – is also evident in *Elles*. However, without a more precise date for the drawing, its relationship with the lithographs remains speculative, although evidence suggests that it was perhaps conceived as a prelude to plates of *Elles*, as well as an autonomous work of art.

The form of Mlle Popo is positioned diagonally across the paper. She lies on a bed beneath a carelessly arranged cover which is tucked under her chin but exposes calves and feet. The head is subtly and precisely modelled with short diagonal strokes of a sharp pencil which indicate shadows around the eyes, cheekbones, nose and lips. A touch of dilute carbon ink or watercolour wash suggests the luminous midtone of flesh to the left of the nose. The waves of the hair are rendered with appropriately freer, cursive strokes, which run into, and are echoed by, the more coarsely drawn folds of the bedclothes. These fan out in a series of 'S' curves, forming a triangular configuration which both stabilises and draws attention to the head. The head's position on the page is ultimately secured by the sinuous creases in the cover, which descend from the corner of Mlle Popo's mouth to the bottom of the composition. Towards the centre of the sheet, the drapery's folds become larger, and are drawn with dislocated and frequently revised strokes. Lightly indicated lines at the composition's centre imply the form of the model's crossed legs beneath the cover, but otherwise the artist's concern here is to establish the plunging perspective of the bedclothes' silhouette.

Counterbalancing the tonal weight of the head, and contrasting with its minutely accurate draughtsmanship, are the legs and feet which thrust dramatically from under the cover. The approximate extent of the heels is hurriedly noted at the extreme right of the sheet, while the limbs themselves are continually redefined by rapid, sweeping contours. The size of the feet (approximately $2\frac{1}{2}$ times that of the head) allied to their handling with loose, open contours, suggests the exaggerated prominence of out-of-focus foreground forms visible in certain photographs. Such perspectival distortions were by the 1890s accepted as part of the formal language of many French avant-garde painters; and Lautrec's interest in, and use of photography, was second only to that of Edgar Degas. Indeed, an undated photograph of Lautrec reclining in a garden chair at Malromé includes the unfocused image of the magnified soles of the artist's boots, the form of which is closely comparable to that of Mlle Popo's feet in this drawing.   w.b.

Paul Cézanne (1839–1906)

Mme Cézanne Sewing c.1880

Pencil; on pale cream wove paper, with laid and chain lines and watermark imitated mechanically, 47.3 × 31

Princes Gate Collection

Probably the earliest drawing of Mme Cézanne sewing appears on a sketchbook page of about 1877–80 which, together with a partial study of the figure of 1879–80, relates to the painting in the Paul Rosenberg Coll., Paris. In the oil, Mme Cézanne sits erect facing right (a reversal of the pose in the drawings) behind a small table: she sews a crisply facetted, fractured triangle of cloth which both generates and supports the major contours of her torso. A wide, high-backed chair creates a curvilinear variation of the body it contains and stabilises. The contours of the top of the chairback coincide with the line of hair across Mme Cézanne's forehead.

The present drawing, of c.1880, reworks with a greater economy of formal means ideas adumbrated in the painting. Only a fragment of the sewing is realised here, and the principal contours constructing the figure echo two dominant triangles found in the body itself. The first, formed by the opening of the jacket over the stomach, is repeated in the fall of the jacket's sides, the position of the upper arms, and the sewn cloth. This triangle's left diagonal is varied in the upper contour of the right forearm and in the curved side of the chairback. The shoulders create the second triangle: creases in the jacket below the right elbow and at the hem, the folds of skirt above and below the left thigh, and the line of skirt projecting from the seat of the chair resonate with the angle of the right shoulder. The line of the left shoulder is echoed by the upper contour of the left forearm, and below, by the crease of the jacket: it too is carried over into motifs adjacent to the figure, such as the topmost book on the cupboard, and the diagonals to the lower right of the chair.

Mme Cézanne is here seen from a higher vantage point than in the painting, and the head, now tilted forward, is located more securely within the torso. The relationship of head to body – strengthened by accents of left eyelid and division of lips which repeat diagonals of the sewing and of the apex of the jacket's opening – is secured by the endboard of a bed against which the figure is posed. But the rhythm of the contour of the endboard is sustained by the positioning of the eyelids. The oval form of the inclined head finds its counterpoint in the shape of the bed-knob; and the subtle oblique angle of the bed-post which is continued through the right side of Mme Cézanne relates her form to the rectilinear structure of cupboard and books at the left of the sheet. These grid-like forms, indicating a pictorial space parallel to the drawing's surface, contrast with the crosspieces of chairback, right, through which background space curves towards the viewer around the axis of Mme Cézanne's body: and through the concave character of background space, those volumes of the body which are hidden from the spectator are implied. w.b.

Paul Cézanne (1839–1906)

Still-life with Apples, Bottle and Chairback 1900–06

Extensive drawing in pencil, both under and over painted areas; gouache; on off-white wove paper, with a watermark imitated mechanically. The sheet unevenly torn, bottom and right, 45.8 × 60.4

Samuel Courtauld Collection

Cézanne's ultimate conception of still-life appears only in his late watercolours. The glass and striped wallpaper here are also those which appear in the watercolour *The Dessert* (Bernheim de Villiers Coll., Paris) also of 1900–6, while the boldly brushed-in chairback has close affinities with *The Rococo Clock* (Kunstmuseum, Basel), possibly one of Cézanne's last works in pencil.

In a letter to Emile Bernard of 25 July 1904, Cézanne defined the patch of paper left bare near the centre of motifs in the watercolours as the 'culminating point' of the form, or that area of the object closest to the eye. In the late watercolours, colours fan out from this point in the logical sequence of the spectrum; and after 1900, hues gain in intensity. The apples here provide a clear illustration of this 'culminating point': from the blank paper emanate, in order, red, yellow and blue. Of the secondary colours, orange is sparingly applied, always between red and yellow, while green, usually juxtaposed with blue, is also introduced into the table top and chairback to activate the reds and browns of these motifs, and to control the placing of fruit and dish.

The arcs of colour interlocking with the white of the paper construct the pile of fruit, contained at the top by the curving crosspiece of the chairback. Within the kidney-shape of the upper chairback, minor areas, supported by freely drawn curves in pencil, palely echo the colours of the bowl of fruit, and possibly represent its reflection in a mirror on the wall behind. Like brushstrokes are grouped in zones which compose the watercolour: towards the centre of the composition, however, all strokes are transformed to resonate with the concentration of arcs in the motifs of bowl, fruit and chairback. The irregular, overlapping patches denoting the extreme left and right of the table's surface are consolidated into strokes whose thinness, length and flexibility increase as they advance towards the fruit dish, curving round its base to suggest a reflection in the table top. Similarly, broad vertical strokes indicating the lateral sides of the wall become shorter and curved as they approach the chairback. At the centre of the table's edge, horizontal strokes of irregular length and thickness are concentrated to support and stabilize the motifs above.

The thickness of gouache describing fruit and leaves – sufficient to create a ridge at the edge of certain brushstrokes – complements both the intensity of colour and indications of volume in these motifs. Cézanne uses, contrastingly, throughout the remainder of the sheet fluid and transparent paint – properties which he exploits to maintain each colour patch's autonomy, and to suggest in all contours, except those in blue, an edge or direction. He achieves this by momentarily resting the brush at either the line's lateral edge, or by tilting the sheet to encourage the flow of paint to specific areas: such directional contours are visible in the crosspiece of the chairback and right side of the bottle. The blue contours, less modified in density and hue, simultaneously create space between the apples and unite them into a compositional wedge: this blue is echoed by paler glides of colour at the top and bottom of the composition. Since no pencil work indicates an original lower position on the sheet for the alignment of apples, right, the blue arcs immediately below may be reflections in the table top of the spaces between the fruit, thus demonstrating a facet of Cézanne's rich imaginative and interpretative vision.   W.B.

Index of Artists